THE CONTROLLER'S PLAYBOOK FOR THE PRIVATE-EQUITY OWNED BUSINESS

Mastering Financial Controllership in PE-Backed Companies for CFOs, Controllers, and FP&A Directors

WILLIAM EROSH

The Controller's Playbook For The Private-Equity Owned Business

Published by:

Divine Creativity LLC

DIVINE CREATIVITY LLC
CREATIVE PUBLISHING SOLUTIONS

TABLE OF CONTENTS

● ◆ ●

INTRODUCTION

● ◆ ●

INTRODUCTION TO FINANCIAL CONTROLLERSHIP IN THE PRIVATE EQUITY OWNED BUSINESS

The role of a financial controller in a private equity (PE)-backed company is both demanding and multifaceted, requiring a unique blend of technical accounting expertise, strategic insight, and operational efficiency. Note that in some companies, duties are split between the controller and the Director of Financial, Planning and Analysis (FP&A). Unlike traditional corporate environments, where financial reporting may follow a more predictable cadence, PE-backed firms operate under heightened scrutiny from investors who demand rapid, accurate, and actionable financial data. The financial controller serves as the linchpin between the company's operational teams and its private equity sponsors, ensuring that financial statements are not only compliant with Generally Accepted Accounting Principles (GAAP) but also structured to support value creation initiatives. We will explore the core responsibilities of a financial controller in this high-stakes environment, the differences between private equity, venture capital, and founder-owned businesses, and the critical skills needed to thrive in this role.

Private equity ownership introduces a distinct set of challenges and expectations. PE firms typically acquire companies with the intent of improving operational performance, optimizing capital structure, and ultimately selling the business at a higher valuation usually within a three-to-seven-year horizon. This aggressive timeline means that financial controllers must be adept at producing real-time financial insights, implementing robust internal controls, and driving process improvements that enhance efficiency. Unlike venture capital (VC)-backed firms, which often prioritize growth over profitability in early stages, or founder-owned businesses, where decision-making may be more decentralized, PE-backed companies require a disciplined approach to financial management. The financial controller must balance the need for compliance and accuracy with the urgency of delivering data that informs strategic decisions—whether that involves cost-cutting measures, revenue optimization, or M&A activity, among other initiatives.

One of the most critical distinctions between private equity, venture capital, and founder-led businesses lies in their investment theses and governance structures. Private equity firms typically acquire mature companies with relatively stable cash flows, using leverage to enhance returns, whereas venture capital focuses on high-growth startups with unproven business models. Founder-owned businesses, on the other hand, may prioritize long-term sustainability over rapid exits, often resulting in less external pressure for financial optimization. The financial controller in a PE-backed company must navigate these dynamics by ensuring that financial reporting aligns with investor expectations, that cash flow is meticulously managed to service debt, and that operational metrics are tracked with precision. This requires not only deep technical knowledge but also the ability to communicate complex financial concepts to non-financial stakeholders, including PE operating partners and board members.

> *The best financial controllers in private equity don't just report the past—they help shape the future by providing the data and insights that drive value creation.*

To excel in this environment, financial controllers must master a broad range of responsibilities, from overseeing the monthly close process to coordinating annual audits, managing treasury functions, and supporting M&A due diligence and other activities. Each of these areas requires a keen eye for detail, a proactive mindset, and the ability to work under tight, and sometimes competing deadlines. Additionally, controllers must stay abreast of evolving accounting standards, tax regulations, and financial reporting requirements, ensuring that the company remains compliant while optimizing its financial performance. We will delve into these responsibilities in greater detail, providing a roadmap for financial professionals looking to succeed in the high-pressure world of private equity-backed companies.

THE FINANCIAL CONTROLLER'S CORE RESPONSIBILITIES

General Accounting and Financial Reporting

At the heart of the financial controller's role is the oversight of general accounting functions, ensuring that all financial transactions are accurately recorded, classified, and reported in accordance with GAAP. This includes managing the month-end and year-end close processes, reconciling balance sheet accounts, and preparing financial statements that provide a true and fair view of the company's financial position. In a private equity-backed company, the close process is often accelerated to meet the demands of investors who require timely insights into performance. Controllers must implement efficient workflows, leverage automation where possible, and maintain rigorous review process to minimize errors and discrepancies. The ability to close the books quickly without sacrificing accuracy is a hallmark of a high-performing controllership function, and it requires close collaboration between accounting teams, FP&A, IT departments, and external auditors.

Beyond the basic bookkeeping functions, financial controllers, in conjunction with the FP&A team, are responsible for ensuring that financial reporting meets the specific needs of private equity sponsors. This often involves preparing customized reports that highlight key performance indicators (KPIs), EBITDA adjustments, debt covenants, and working capital trends. PE investors are particularly focused on cash flow generation, leverage ratios, and operational efficiency, so controllers must design reporting packages that align with these priorities. Additionally, controllers play a critical role in coordinating the annual financial audit, serving as the primary liaison between the company and its external auditors. This includes preparing audit schedules, addressing auditor inquiries, and ensuring that any material weaknesses or deficiencies in internal controls are promptly remediated. The audit process in a PE-backed company is often more rigorous than in other environments, as investors and lenders rely on audited financials to assess the company's health and compliance with debt covenants.

Treasury Management and Cash Flow Forecasting

Effective treasury management is another cornerstone of the financial controller's responsibilities, particularly in leveraged environments where cash flow is closely monitored. Controllers must oversee cash positioning, manage banking relationships, and ensure that the company maintains adequate liquidity to meet its obligations. This includes forecasting short-term and long-term cash needs, optimizing working capital, and implementing strategies to reduce interest expenses. In private equity, where companies often carry significant debt, the ability to accurately predict cash flow is essential for avoiding liquidity crunches and maintaining investor confidence. Controllers must work closely with the CFO and operational leaders to develop rolling cash flow forecasts that account for seasonality, capital expenditures, and debt service requirements.

Cash flow forecasting in a PE-backed company is not just about predicting future balances—it's about identifying opportunities to improve cash conversion cycles and reduce inefficiencies. For example, controllers may analyze accounts receivable aging reports to identify late-paying customers and implement stricter collections policies, or they may negotiate extended payment terms with suppliers to preserve cash. Additionally, controllers must ensure that the company complies with any cash sweep provisions in its credit agreements, which may require excess cash to be used for debt repayment. The ability to balance operational needs with financial constraints is a key differentiator for successful controllers in this space.

Budgeting, Forecasting, and Performance Management

Budgeting and forecasting are critical tools for private equity-backed companies, as they provide a roadmap for achieving the financial targets set by investors. The financial controller, usually with the FP&A team, plays a central role in developing annual budgets, long-range plans, and periodic forecasts that align with the company's strategic objectives. This involves collaborating with department heads to gather input, validating assumptions, and ensuring that budgets are both ambitious and achievable. In many cases, PE sponsors will set aggressive growth or margin improvement targets, and the controller must ensure that the financial plan supports these goals while remaining grounded in reality.

Once the budget is finalized, the controller is responsible for tracking performance against plan, identifying variances, and providing actionable insights to management. This often involves preparing monthly or quarterly performance reports that compare actual results to budgeted figures, highlighting areas of over- or under-performance. In a private equity context, these reports are not just internal tools—they are shared with investors and lenders, who use them to assess the company's progress and make decisions about additional capital injections or operational interventions. Controllers must therefore ensure that forecasts are dynamic, incorporating the latest business trends and adjusting for unforeseen challenges such as economic downturns or supply chain disruptions.

Mergers, Acquisitions, and Divestitures

Private equity firms frequently engage in mergers and acquisitions (M&A) as a means of driving growth and creating value. The financial controller is a key player in these transactions, providing critical support during due diligence, financial modeling, and post-merger integration. On the buy side, controllers must assess the target company's financial statements, identify potential accounting or tax risks, and ensure that the acquisition is structured in a way that aligns with the buyer's strategic objectives. This often involves working closely with external advisors, including investment bankers, legal counsel, and tax specialists, to evaluate the target's financial health and uncover any hidden liabilities. Post-transaction, controllers play a pivotal role in integrating acquired businesses, harmonizing accounting policies, consolidating financial systems, and ensuring that synergies are captured.

On the sell side, controllers are responsible for preparing the company or subsidiary for sale by ensuring that financial records are clean, GAAP-compliant, and presented in a way that maximizes valuation. This may involve recasting financial statements to normalize EBITDA, addressing any audit findings, and preparing data rooms for potential buyers. The ability to navigate the complexities of M&A is a defining skill for financial controllers in private equity, as these transactions often have a material impact on the company's financial trajectory.

7

Internal Controls, Compliance, and Financial Systems

Strong internal controls are essential for mitigating risk, preventing fraud, and ensuring the accuracy of financial reporting. In a private equity-backed company, where investors demand transparency and accountability, the financial controller must design, implement, and monitor control frameworks that safeguard assets and ensure compliance with regulatory requirements. This includes segregation of duties, approval hierarchies, and periodic audits of high-risk areas such as accounts payable and payroll. Controllers must also stay abreast of evolving accounting standards (e.g., ASC 606 for revenue recognition or ASC 842 for leases) and ensure that the company's policies are timely updated accordingly.

In addition to controls, financial controllers are often tasked with evaluating and optimizing the company's financial systems. Many PE-backed companies operate on legacy systems that are inefficient or lack the scalability needed to support growth. Controllers must assess whether upgrading to an ERP system (e.g., NetSuite, SAP, Intacct or Oracle) would improve reporting capabilities, reduce manual work, and enhance data accuracy. Implementing new systems requires careful planning, stakeholder buy-in, and change management to ensure a smooth transition. The ability to leverage technology to drive efficiency is becoming increasingly important in modern controllership, particularly in fast-paced private equity environments where data-driven decision-making is paramount.

KEY POINTS

The role of a financial controller in a private equity-backed company is both challenging and rewarding, requiring a unique combination of technical expertise, strategic thinking, and operational acumen. From overseeing GAAP-compliant financial reporting to managing treasury functions, supporting M&A activity, and strengthening internal controls, controllers are at the center of value creation in these high-performance organizations. By mastering these responsibilities and understanding the distinct dynamics of private equity ownership, financial professionals can position themselves as indispensable partners to both management teams and investors. The remaining chapters of this book will delve a little deeper into each of these areas, providing actionable insights and best practices for excelling in the world of private equity controllership.

CHAPTER 1:

THE PRIVATE EQUITY LANDSCAPE

• ◆ •

UNDERSTANDING OWNERSHIP STRUCTURES: PRIVATE EQUITY, VENTURE CAPITAL, AND FOUNDER-OWNED BUSINESSES

The financial controller's role varies significantly depending on the ownership structure of the company. Private equity, venture capital, and founder-owned businesses each impose distinct financial reporting, compliance, and operational demands. Private equity firms acquire mature companies, often with significant debt, and focus on operational improvements and eventual exits through sales or IPOs. Venture capital, on the other hand, invests in high-growth startups, prioritizing scalability over immediate profitability, which means financial controllers in VC-backed firms must manage burn rates and investor reporting with precision. Founder-owned businesses, while more flexible, often lack the rigorous financial infrastructure of PE or VC-backed firms, requiring controllers to build processes from the ground up.

Private equity ownership is characterized by leveraged buyouts (LBOs), where the acquired company's cash flows service the debt used to purchase it. This structure demands meticulous cash flow management, stringent cost controls, and frequent reporting to PE sponsors who expect detailed performance metrics. Venture capital-backed companies, meanwhile, operate under a high-risk, high-reward model where financial controllers must balance aggressive growth targets with the need to extend runway between funding rounds. Founder-owned businesses may not face the same external pressures but often struggle with informal processes, requiring controllers to implement GAAP compliant frameworks.

> *The difference between private equity and venture capital isn't just about the stage of investment—it's about the entire financial and operational philosophy driving the business.*

Key distinctions include:

- Investment Horizon: PE firms typically hold investments for 3–7 years, while VC firms may stay invested for 5–10 years or until an exit event.

- Leverage Usage: PE relies heavily on debt; VC uses equity financing.

- Reporting Requirements: PE demands monthly or quarterly EBITDA targets; VC focuses on growth metrics like customer acquisition cost (CAC) and lifetime value (LTV).

- Exit Strategies: PE seeks IPOs or strategic sales; VC looks for acquisitions or public offerings.

- Operational Involvement: PE sponsors often install management teams; VCs take board seats but rarely intervene in daily operations.

Understanding these differences is critical for financial controllers, as they dictate the cadence of financial reporting, the level of detail required, and the strategic priorities that must be reflected in financial statements.

THE FINANCIAL CONTROLLER'S ROLE IN PRIVATE EQUITY-BACKED COMPANIES

In a private equity-owned company, the financial controller is the linchpin between operational execution and investor expectations. Unlike in public companies, where quarterly earnings dominate, PE-backed firms require real-time visibility into financials to support rapid decision-making. The controller must ensure that monthly closes are not just accurate but also insightful, providing the PE sponsor with actionable data on EBITDA margins, working capital efficiency, and covenant compliance. Since PE firms often use debt financing, controllers must also monitor leverage ratios and debt service coverage to avoid covenant breaches that could trigger lender interventions.

Another critical responsibility is assisting in managing the "100-day plan" post-acquisition, where the PE firm will likely expect immediate cost rationalization and process improvements. Controllers must quickly identify redundancies, implement tighter controls, and align accounting policies with the sponsor's standards. This often involves integrating newly acquired entities into existing financial systems, harmonizing chart of accounts, and ensuring that intercompany transactions are properly eliminated in consolidations. Given the high stakes, controllers in PE environments must be adept at balancing short-term financial engineering with long-term value creation.

Cash flow forecasting takes on heightened importance in PE-owned companies because sponsors prioritize free cash flow (FCF) as a key metric. Controllers must develop reliable rolling 13-week cash flow models that account for seasonality, capital expenditures, and debt repayments. These forecasts are scrutinized during quarterly board meetings, where deviations from projections require immediate explanations and corrective actions. Additionally, controllers often collaborate with PE operating partners to implement zero-based budgeting, ensuring that every dollar spent aligns with strategic objectives.

Internal controls in a PE setting must be robust enough to satisfy not only auditors but also the sponsor's due diligence teams. Controllers should expect frequent audits—both financial and operational—as PE firms seek to validate performance and uncover hidden inefficiencies. This environment demands a proactive approach to control design, including segregation of duties, automated approval workflows, and regular fraud risk assessments. Given the pressure to deliver exits, controllers must also prepare carve-out financials for potential divestitures, ensuring that discontinued operations are cleanly separated for reporting purposes.

THE UNIQUE CHALLENGES OF VENTURE CAPITAL-BACKED COMPANIES

Venture capital-backed companies present a different set of challenges for financial controllers, primarily due to their focus on growth over profitability. Unlike PE-owned firms, where EBITDA is king, VC-backed startups prioritize metrics like monthly recurring revenue (MRR), churn rate, and gross margin scalability. Controllers must design financial reporting frameworks that capture these non-GAAP metrics while still maintaining compliance with traditional accounting standards. This dual reporting requirement can strain resources, especially in early-stage companies where finance teams are lean.

Cash burn rate is a critical concern in VC-backed firms (as well as PE-backed ones), and controllers must implement stringent cash management practices to extend runway between funding rounds. This involves:

- Weekly cash position tracking to avoid liquidity shortfalls.

- Scenario modeling for different growth trajectories.

- Investor reporting packages that highlight key performance indicators (KPIs) like CAC payback periods.

- Cap table management to ensure accurate equity dilution tracking.

- 409A valuations for stock option and/or profit interest unit grants.

Since VC investors often sit on the board, controllers must prepare board decks that succinctly explain financial performance in the context of growth milestones. These materials must bridge the gap between GAAP financials and the operational metrics that VCs care about, such as product development timelines and market penetration rates. Controllers also play a key role in fundraising, preparing data rooms for due diligence and ensuring that financial projections are both ambitious and defensible.

Tax compliance in VC-backed companies can be complex, particularly when dealing with R\&D tax credits, international expansion, or multi-state nexus issues. Controllers must navigate these complexities while also managing the expectations of investors who may prioritize growth over tax efficiency. Transfer pricing becomes a concern once startups expand globally, requiring controllers to document intercompany agreements and ensure compliance with OECD guidelines. Additionally, the use of stock-based compensation necessitates careful accounting under ASC 718, with controllers ensuring that expense recognition aligns with vesting schedules.

FOUNDER-OWNED BUSINESSES: BUILDING FINANCIAL DISCIPLINE FROM THE GROUND UP

Founder-owned businesses often lack the formalized financial infrastructure of PE or VC-backed firms, presenting both opportunities and challenges for controllers. In these environments, the controller's first task is usually to transition from cash-based or tax-basis accounting to full GAAP compliance. This involves educating founders on the importance of accruals, revenue recognition principles, and the balance between tax minimization and financial transparency. Unlike PE or VC settings, where external investors drive reporting standards, controllers in founder-led firms must advocate for best practices while respecting the owner's vision.

One of the biggest hurdles in founder-owned companies is implementing internal controls without stifling entrepreneurial agility. Controllers must design controls that mitigate risks—such as fraud or misreporting—while allowing the business to remain nimble. This might involve:

- Segregation of duties even in small teams by leveraging outsourced services.

- Automated approval workflows for expenditures above certain thresholds.

- Regular reconciliations to catch discrepancies early.

- Fraud risk assessments tailored to the company's specific vulnerabilities.

- Founder training on financial literacy to ensure buy-in.

Budgeting in founder-owned businesses is often less formalized, requiring controllers to introduce rolling forecasts that adapt to changing market conditions. Unlike PE firms with rigid quarterly targets, founder-led companies may prioritize reinvestment over short-term profitability, necessitating flexible financial planning tools. Controllers must also manage the tension between the founder's personal financial interests—such as owner draws or related-party transactions—and the need for transparent corporate financials.

Tax strategy in founder-owned businesses can be highly personalized, with controllers balancing entity structuring (e.g., S-corps vs. LLCs), state tax optimization, and succession planning. Unlike VC or PE-backed firms, where tax strategy is often standardized, founder-owned companies may require bespoke solutions to align with the owner's long-term goals. Controllers must also prepare for eventual ownership transitions, whether through generational transfers, ESOPs, or sales to financial buyers, each of which demands different financial and tax preparations.

KEY TAKEAWAYS FOR CONTROLLERS ACROSS OWNERSHIP MODELS

Regardless of ownership structure, financial controllers must adapt their approach to meet the unique demands of their stakeholders. In private equity, the emphasis is on precision, speed, and leverage management; in venture capital, it's about growth metrics and runway extension; in founder-owned businesses, it's balancing formality with flexibility. Controllers who understand these nuances can position themselves as strategic partners rather than mere number-crunchers.

The most successful controllers proactively align their teams with ownership priorities, whether that means implementing PE-style dashboards, building VC-friendly KPI reports, or educating founder-owners on GAAP compliance. They also stay ahead of regulatory changes—such as new revenue recognition standards or tax laws—that could impact financial reporting. Above all, they recognize that their role isn't just about historical accuracy but about shaping the financial future of the business.

> *A great financial controller doesn't just report the numbers—they translate them into the language of their audience, whether that's a PE sponsor, a VC board member, or a founder-CEO.*

By mastering the intricacies of each ownership model, controllers can drive value far beyond the accounting department, becoming indispensable allies in the pursuit of financial and operational excellence.

CHAPTER 2:

GAAP COMPLIANCE AND FINANCIAL REPORTING

● ◆ ●

THE PILLARS OF FINANCIAL INTEGRITY

Adhering to Generally Accepted Accounting Principles is the bedrock of financial controllership. GAAP provides a standardized framework that ensures consistency, comparability, and transparency in financial reporting. For private equity-owned companies, GAAP compliance is not just a regulatory requirement—it is a critical component of investor confidence, lender trust, and operational credibility. The financial controller plays a pivotal role in interpreting and implementing these principles, ensuring that every transaction, disclosure, and financial statement aligns with the prescribed guidelines.

GAAP compliance begins with a deep understanding of the Financial Accounting Standards Board (FASB) pronouncements, including Accounting Standards Codification (ASC) topics. Controllers must stay abreast of evolving standards, such as revenue recognition (ASC 606), lease accounting (ASC 842), and fair value measurements (ASC 820). These standards dictate how transactions are recorded, measured, and disclosed, directly impacting financial statements. For example, ASC 606 requires companies to recognize revenue when performance obligations are satisfied, which may necessitate changes to billing cycles, contract reviews, and revenue deferral policies.

Beyond technical knowledge, GAAP compliance demands rigorous internal controls. Controllers must establish processes to prevent misstatements, detect errors, and ensure timely corrections. This includes segregation of duties, reconciliation procedures, and approval hierarchies. A lapse in controls can lead to material misstatements, audit qualifications, or even regulatory penalties. Private equity sponsors, in particular, scrutinize these controls during due diligence, as weaknesses can devalue a company or trigger post-acquisition remediation costs.

The financial reporting cycle under GAAP is methodical. Monthly closes require accruals, deferrals, and adjustments to reflect the true financial position. Year-end closes involve additional complexities, such as footnote disclosures, segment reporting, and equity roll-forwards. Controllers must balance speed with accuracy, as delayed reporting can erode stakeholder trust. For private equity-owned firms, monthly and/or quarterly reporting to sponsors adds another layer of urgency, often with tighter deadlines than public companies.

GAAP is not just about rules—it's about telling the financial story of a company with clarity and precision. A controller's ability to translate complex transactions into compliant financials is what separates good finance teams from great ones.

GAAP VS. NON-GAAP METRICS: STRIKING THE RIGHT BALANCE

While GAAP provides uniformity, companies often supplement their reporting with non-GAAP metrics like EBITDA, adjusted net income, or free cash flow. These metrics offer insights into operational performance by excluding one-time items, non-cash expenses, or other "noise." However, controllers must navigate this practice carefully. Over-reliance on non-GAAP measures can mislead stakeholders, while ignoring them may obscure key performance drivers.

Private equity sponsors frequently prioritize non-GAAP metrics to evaluate portfolio companies. For instance, EBITDA is a cornerstone for valuation multiples and debt covenants. Controllers must ensure these metrics are derived from GAAP figures and clearly reconciled in footnotes. The SEC's Regulation G mandates that non-GAAP measures must not be presented more prominently than GAAP measures, and adjustments must be justified. A common pitfall is "cherry-picking" adjustments to inflate performance, which can trigger regulatory scrutiny or lender disputes.

Documentation is critical when using non-GAAP metrics. Controllers should maintain policies defining each metric, calculation methodologies, and the business rationale for adjustments. During audits, these policies are scrutinized for consistency and transparency. For example, if a company excludes restructuring costs from EBITDA, it must apply this definition uniformly across periods and disclose the nature of these costs.

In mergers and acquisitions, non-GAAP adjustments often arise in quality of earnings (QoE) reports. Buyers may normalize earnings by adding back owner-related expenses or non-recurring items. Controllers involved in sell-side due diligence must ensure these adjustments are supportable and defensible. Misalignment between GAAP and non-GAAP figures can derail negotiations or lead to post-close purchase price adjustments.

- Define non-GAAP metrics in written policies

- Reconcile non-GAAP measures to GAAP figures

- Ensure consistency in adjustments across reporting periods

- Disclose the rationale for excluding specific items

- Train management on compliant non-GAAP communication

FINANCIAL REPORTING FOR PRIVATE EQUITY SPONSORS AND LENDERS

Private equity-owned companies face unique reporting demands. Sponsors require granular, timely data to monitor investments, while lenders impose strict covenant reporting. Controllers must tailor financial statements to meet these dual objectives without compromising GAAP integrity.

THE CONTROLLER'S PLAYBOOK

Sponsor reporting often includes:

- Flash reports: High-level summaries of monthly performance, delivered within days of period close.

- Dashboards: KPIs like revenue growth, gross margin trends, and working capital ratios.

- Portfolio reviews: Deep dives into segment performance, prepared quarterly for investment committees.

Lenders, on the other hand, focus on covenant compliance. Debt agreements typically specify GAAP-based metrics such as leverage ratios (debt/EBITDA) or interest coverage (EBIT/interest expense). Controllers must ensure calculations align with loan definitions, which may differ from internal metrics. For example, EBITDA for covenants might exclude capital expenditures below a certain threshold, requiring precise tracking.

Timeliness is paramount. Late or inaccurate covenant reporting can trigger defaults, even if the company is performing well operationally. Controllers should establish a checklist for covenant packages:

- Verify calculation methodologies per the credit agreement

- Obtain sign-off from legal, the CFO and the PE operating team before submission

- Archive supporting documentation for audits

- Monitor "cushion" levels to anticipate breaches

- Coordinate with treasury to align cash flow forecasts

For multi-entity portfolios, consolidations add complexity. Intercompany transactions must be identified and eliminated, and foreign subsidiaries' results translated under ASC 830. Controllers should implement systems to automate eliminations and ensure compliance with the equity method or full consolidation rules.

THE AUDIT LIFECYCLE: FROM PLANNING TO REMEDIATION

Annual audits are a cornerstone of GAAP compliance. For private equity-backed firms, audits validate financials for sponsors, lenders, and potential buyers. Controllers orchestrate this process, liaising between auditors, management, and external stakeholders.

Audit planning begins months in advance. Controllers should:

- Assess risk areas: Identify high-risk accounts (e.g., revenue, goodwill) and complex transactions (e.g., derivatives, M&A).

- Prepare schedules: Compile trial balances, reconciliations, and supporting documents.

- Coordinate with auditors: Align on timelines, materiality thresholds, and sampling methods.

During fieldwork, auditors test controls and substantiate balances. Common pain points include:

- Revenue recognition: Auditors scrutinize contract terms to verify ASC 606 compliance.

- Inventory obsolescence: Reserves must be backed by aging reports and historical write-off trends.

- Management estimates: Fair value assessments (e.g., for intangible assets) require robust documentation.

Post-audit, controllers address findings through "management letter comments." Remediation might involve:

- Enhancing controls (e.g., implementing dual approvals for journal entries).

- Revising policies (e.g., updating capitalization thresholds for fixed assets).

- Training staff on new procedures.

An audit is not a pass/fail test—it's an opportunity to strengthen financial processes. The best controllers treat auditor feedback as a roadmap for continuous improvement.

TECHNOLOGY'S ROLE IN GAAP COMPLIANCE

Modern financial systems are indispensable for GAAP compliance. ERP platforms (e.g., NetSuite, SAP, Intacct) automate journal entries, consolidations, and reporting, reducing manual errors. Controllers should prioritize:

- System configurations: Ensure the chart of accounts aligns with GAAP classifications (e.g., separating operating vs. financing leases post-ASC 842).

- Integration: Link and robustly maintain subledgers (AP, AR, deferred revenue, payroll) to the general ledger for real-time data flow.

- Audit trails: Maintain logs of user activity to satisfy SOX requirements.

Emerging technologies like AI can flag anomalies in real-time (e.g., duplicate payments or unusual revenue patterns). Blockchain can offer potential for immutable transaction records.

For private equity roll-ups, controllers must harmonize systems across acquired entities. This includes standardizing:

- Account structures

- Close calendars

- Reporting templates

- Control frameworks

Ultimately, technology is an enabler—but human oversight remains irreplaceable. Controllers must validate system outputs and retain accountability for GAAP adherence.

KEY POINTS

GAAP compliance and financial reporting are not static obligations but dynamic disciplines that require technical expertise, meticulous controls, and strategic communication. For controllers in private equity environments, mastering these areas is essential to driving transparency, maintaining stakeholder trust, and positioning their companies for successful exits. By embracing both the rules and the spirit of GAAP, financial leaders can turn compliance into a competitive advantage.

CHAPTER 3:

MONTHLY AND YEAR-END CLOSE PROCESSES

● ◆ ●

THE MONTHLY AND YEAR-END CLOSE PROCESSES

The monthly and year-end close processes are the backbone of financial controllership. These cycles ensure that financial statements are accurate, compliant, and timely—critical for internal decision-making, external reporting, and maintaining stakeholder confidence. A well-structured close process minimizes errors, reduces last-minute fire drills, and provides a clear financial snapshot of the business. For private equity-owned companies, the stakes are even higher: investors demand precision, transparency, and speed to assess performance against targets. This chapter addresses some of the most important best practices for streamlining these processes, addressing common pitfalls, and aligning them with the unique demands of private equity oversight.

THE IMPORTANCE OF A STRUCTURED CLOSE PROCESS

A disciplined close process is not just about ticking boxes—it's about creating a reliable foundation for strategic decisions. Private equity sponsors, lenders, and management teams rely on accurate financials to evaluate performance, covenant compliance, and investment returns. A poorly executed close can lead to misinformed decisions, audit findings, or even breaches of loan agreements. The close process also serves as a control mechanism, ensuring that all financial activities—revenue recognition, expense accruals, reconciliations—are properly recorded and reviewed. Without structure, discrepancies can snowball into material misstatements, eroding trust with stakeholders.

One of the biggest challenges in the close process is balancing speed and accuracy. Private equity firms often impose tight reporting deadlines, sometimes requiring preliminary numbers within five business days of month-end. This urgency can pressure teams to cut corners, but automation, standardized workflows, and clear role assignments can mitigate risks. Another critical factor is cross-departmental collaboration. Finance doesn't operate in a vacuum; operations, sales, and procurement must provide timely data. Establishing a close calendar with firm deadlines for each department ensures accountability and prevents bottlenecks.

> *A smooth close isn't about working harder—it's about working smarter. Automation, checklists, and a disciplined timeline turn chaos into control.*

Technology plays a pivotal role in modern close processes. Cloud-based accounting systems, robotic process automation, and AI-driven reconciliation tools reduce manual effort and human error. For example, automated journal entries for recurring transactions (e.g., depreciation, lease accounting) save hours of repetitive work. Similarly, reconciliation software can flag discrepancies in real time, allowing teams to resolve issues before the close deadline. However, technology is only as good as the processes it supports. Controllers must ensure that system configurations align with GAAP and that staff are trained to use these tools effectively.

Finally, the close process should be iterative. Post-close reviews help identify inefficiencies. Did the team struggle with inventory reconciliations? Were there delays in intercompany settlements? What components of the process can be performed prior to the close date? Documenting these pain points and refining procedures for the next cycle fosters continuous improvement. In private equity environments, where portfolio companies may face add-on acquisitions or divestitures, scalability is key. A well-documented close process ensures that new entities can be integrated seamlessly into financial reporting.

PRE-CLOSE PREPARATION: LAYING THE GROUNDWORK

The close doesn't start on the last day of the month—it begins weeks in advance. Proactive preparation is the difference between a frantic scramble and a methodical process. One of the first steps is updating the close checklist, a living document that outlines every task, responsible party, and deadline. This checklist should be tailored to the company's specific needs but generally includes account reconciliations, variance analyses, and management review steps. For private equity-owned firms, additional items like covenant calculations or investor reporting templates may be included.

Communication is equally critical. A pre-close meeting with department heads ensures everyone understands their responsibilities. For instance, the sales team must confirm all revenue is recorded, while procurement verifies that accruals for received-but-unbilled goods are accurate. These meetings also surface potential issues early, such as a large customer delaying payment or an unexpected expense spike. Another preparatory step is reviewing open items from the prior close. Unresolved discrepancies or pending adjustments should be flagged and assigned to avoid carryover. I have found it helpful to have quick daily stand-ups during the close itself, in order to ensure that all participants are are aware of status, gating items and issues.

Data integrity checks are another pillar of pre-close work. This includes verifying that sub-ledgers (e.g., accounts payable, accounts receivable) tie to the general ledger and that system interfaces are functioning correctly. For companies with multiple entities, ensuring intercompany transactions are properly recorded eliminates consolidation headaches later. Some controllers also run preliminary analytics, such as trend analysis or ratio checks, to spot anomalies before formal closing begins.

For year-end closes, preparation is even more rigorous. Key tasks include:

- Confirming inventory count schedules

- Coordinating with external auditors on timing and document requests

- Reviewing tax accruals and deferred tax balances

- Validating equity and debt schedules for footnote disclosures

- Testing new accounting standards or policy changes

Private equity sponsors often require "flash reports" or early estimates of key metrics (e.g., EBITDA, cash flow). Establishing a process for these preliminary numbers—without compromising accuracy—is essential. Some firms use a "soft close" around the 25th of the month to capture approximately 80% of expected activity, allowing for quicker high-level reporting.

EXECUTING THE MONTH-END CLOSE

The core of the close process revolves around accuracy, timeliness, and compliance. Day 1 typically involves finalizing revenue recognition if possible (if the revenue process is billing reliant this could cause revenue recognition to be finalized later in the close cycle), ensuring all invoices are posted, and reconciling cash accounts. Revenue is particularly sensitive, especially for companies with complex billing terms or deferred revenue arrangements. Controllers must verify that revenue aligns with contractual terms and that any unbilled receivables (e.g., services performed but not yet invoiced) are accrued. For expense recognition, the focus is on completeness. This means reviewing purchase orders, vendor invoices, and credit card statements to capture all obligations, even if bills haven't been received.

Accruals and prepaids are another layer of scrutiny. Common examples include:

- Payroll accruals for wages earned but not yet paid

- Bonuses or commissions pending final calculation

- Rent, utilities, or subscriptions spanning multiple periods

- Capitalized costs (e.g., software development) requiring amortization

Reconciliations are the backbone of a clean close. Every balance sheet account should be reconciled, with discrepancies investigated and resolved. High-risk areas like cash, accounts receivable, and inventory often require additional scrutiny. For cash, this means matching bank statements to the ledger and investigating uncleared checks or deposits in transit. For receivables, aging reports should be reviewed for collectability, with appropriate bad debt reserves booked. Inventory reconciliations may involve physical counts or system-generated reports, adjusted for obsolescence or shrinkage.

Intercompany transactions add complexity, especially for multi-entity structures. Eliminations must be accurate to avoid double-counting revenue or expenses. Best practices include:

- Maintaining a centralized intercompany ledger

- Requiring monthly confirmation between entities

- Standardizing exchange rates for foreign transactions

- Documenting intercompany agreements for transfer pricing compliance

By Day 3-4, the focus shifts to preliminary financial statements. The controller reviews the trial balance for unusual entries, such as unexpected variances in expense accounts or imbalances in equity movements. Variance analysis against budget or prior periods helps identify outliers—for example, a sudden drop in gross margin might signal unrecorded costs or pricing errors. For private equity reporting, EBITDA adjustments (e.g., add-backs for one-time expenses) must be well-documented and supportable.

YEAR-END CLOSE AND AUDIT READINESS

The year-end close shares most of the steps with the monthly process but includes additional compliance and reporting requirements. One major difference is the involvement of external auditors, who will test transactions, confirm balances, and opine on financial statements. To streamline the audit, controllers should prepare "audit-ready" workpapers—clearly organized files with reconciliations, supporting documents, and explanatory notes. A best practice is to structure workpapers so that auditors can follow the logic without additional explanations, reducing back-and-forth queries.

Tax provisions are another year-end priority. This includes:

- Calculating current and deferred tax liabilities

- Reviewing state apportionment data for multi-state filings

- Ensuring all tax elections (e.g., bonus depreciation) are properly applied

- Coordinating with external tax advisors on complex issues like R\&D credits or international tax structures

Footnotes and disclosures require meticulous attention. GAAP mandates detailed notes on topics like lease obligations, pension plans, or litigation contingencies. Private equity-owned companies may also need to disclose related-party transactions (e.g., management fees paid to the sponsor or potentially other portfolio company's owned by the PE firm). Drafting these early allows time for legal or auditor review.

For companies undergoing mergers or divestitures, year-end closes can be especially challenging. ASC 805 valuations and purchase price accounting must be done, reviewed and agreed with the auditors. Acquired businesses must be integrated into financial systems, with opening balance sheets aligned to the buyer's accounting policies. Divestitures require carve-out financials, separating the sold entity's results from the parent company. Both scenarios demand careful tracking of purchase price adjustments, working capital settlements, and transition service agreements.

POST-CLOSE ACTIVITIES AND CONTINUOUS IMPROVEMENT

The close isn't truly complete until post-close reviews and stakeholder reporting are finished. For private equity sponsors, this often means preparing a detailed investor package with:

- Financial statements (P&L, balance sheet, cash flow)

- Key performance indicators like customer churn or unit economics

- Covenant compliance calculations (e.g., leverage ratios)

- Management commentary on variances and outlook

Internally, a close retrospective meeting can help identify process improvements. Questions to ask include:

- Were there recurring errors that could be prevented with automation?

- Did any departments consistently delay submissions?

- Were there system limitations that hindered efficiency?

Documenting these lessons and updating procedures ensures each close becomes smoother than the last. For controllers in private equity environments, this cycle of refinement is critical—investors expect not just accuracy, but also scalability as the business grows or undergoes further transactions, perhaps a future IPO which brings on further scrutiny.

> *The close process is a mirror of the finance team's discipline. A clean close reflects a team that controls the numbers, rather than being controlled by them.*

Finally, training and cross-training team members prevents bottlenecks. If only one person knows how to reconcile a complex account, the close is vulnerable to delays. Creating backup coverage and documentation for all critical tasks ensures resilience. Over time, the goal is to shift from a "close" mentality to a "continuous accounting" approach, where real-time data and automation minimize the traditional end-of-month crunch. This evolution is especially valuable for private equity portfolio companies, where agility and transparency are paramount to investor confidence.

CHAPTER 4:

FINANCIAL REPORTING TO PE SPONSORS AND LENDERS

● ◆ ●

FINANCIAL REPORTING FOR PRIVATE EQUITY SPONSORS AND LENDERS

Financial reporting is the backbone of transparency and trust between a company and its stakeholders, particularly private equity sponsors and lenders. Unlike traditional corporate environments, PE-backed companies demand a higher level of precision, timeliness, and strategic insight in their financial reports. This chapter delves into the nuances of financial reporting frameworks tailored for PE sponsors and lenders, covering best practices, common pitfalls, and the critical differences between reporting for private equity versus other ownership structures.

> In private equity, financial reporting isn't just about compliance—it's about storytelling. Your numbers must articulate the company's trajectory, risks, and opportunities in a way that aligns with investor expectations.

UNDERSTANDING THE AUDIENCE: PE SPONSORS VS. LENDERS

Private equity sponsors and lenders have distinct priorities when reviewing financial reports. PE sponsors are focused on value creation, growth metrics, and exit strategies, while lenders prioritize debt service coverage, liquidity, and covenant compliance. A financial controller must tailor reports to address these divergent needs without sacrificing accuracy or consistency.

PE sponsors, for instance, require detailed EBITDA adjustments, working capital trends, and KPIs tied to operational performance. They often request flash reports or dashboards that highlight progress against milestones, such as revenue growth or cost-saving initiatives. Lenders, on the other hand, scrutinize cash flow statements, leverage ratios, and debt maturity schedules to assess repayment capacity. Missing a covenant threshold—such as a debt-to-EBITDA ratio—can trigger penalties or renegotiations, making lender reports a high-stakes deliverable.

Another key difference is the frequency and depth of reporting. While quarterly audited statements may suffice for public companies, PE sponsors often require monthly or even weekly updates, especially during periods of restructuring or rapid growth. Lenders may require quarterly compliance certificates alongside annual audits. Striking the right balance between granularity and conciseness is an art—one that separates effective controllers from the rest.

To streamline reporting, many PE-backed companies adopt investor-grade financial models that integrate GAAP reporting with management adjustments. These models often include scenario analyses (e.g., base case, upside, downside) to help sponsors evaluate exit valuations or refinancing options. For lenders, embedding covenant calculations directly into financial statements reduces the risk of misinterpretation.

- Identify the primary stakeholders (PE sponsors, senior lenders, mezzanine debt providers).

- Segment reports by audience (e.g., operational KPIs for sponsors, liquidity analysis for lenders).

- Standardize templates to ensure consistency across periods.

- Automate covenant tracking to flag breaches proactively.

- Schedule pre-submission reviews with leadership to align messaging.

KEY COMPONENTS OF PE FINANCIAL REPORTS

A well-structured financial report for private equity goes beyond GAAP compliance. It must bridge accounting data with strategic insights, providing sponsors with a clear line of sight into value drivers. Below are the critical components:

Executive Summary

A succinct narrative tying financial results to business performance. For example, if revenue grew by 15% but margins contracted, explain whether this was due to market expansion (a positive) or rising input costs (a risk).

Adjusted EBITDA Reconciliation

PE firms rely on EBITDA as a proxy for cash flow. Adjustments for non-recurring items (e.g., restructuring costs, owner expenses) must be transparent and well-documented. Over-aggressive add-backs can erode credibility.

Working Capital Analysis

Sponsors monitor days sales outstanding (DSO), inventory turnover, and accounts payable cycles to assess operational efficiency. Unexpected swings may signal deeper issues, such as customer concentration or supply chain disruptions.

Capital Expenditures (CapEx) vs. Maintenance Spend

Break down CapEx into growth-related vs. maintenance categories. Lenders want assurance that borrowings fund revenue-generating projects, not just keeping the lights on.

Debt and Liquidity Position

Include a rolling 13-week cash flow forecast to demonstrate short-term liquidity. For lenders, detail compliance with leverage ratios, interest coverage, and any contingent liabilities.

LENDER REPORTING: COVENANTS AND COMPLIANCE

Debt agreements often include financial covenants—performance thresholds that borrowers must maintain. Common covenants include:

- Leverage Ratio (Debt/EBITDA): Typically must stay below 3.5x–4x.

- Interest Coverage Ratio (EBITDA/Interest Expense): Usually a minimum of 2.5x.

- Fixed Charge Coverage Ratio: Measures ability to cover debt payments and leases.

Missing a covenant can lead to defaults, higher interest rates, or forced equity injections. To mitigate risks:

- Model Covenant Scenarios: Stress-test ratios under pessimistic assumptions (e.g., a 10% revenue decline).

- Early Warning Systems: Flag trends (e.g., declining EBITDA margins) before they breach thresholds.

- Negotiate Cure Periods: Some agreements allow a quarter to rectify breaches.

Lenders also require borrowing base certificates for asset-backed loans (e.g., receivables or inventory financing). Controllers must reconcile collateral values with ledger balances and aging reports.

TECHNOLOGY AND AUTOMATION IN REPORTING

Manual reporting processes are prone to errors and inefficiencies. PE-backed firms increasingly adopt ERP systems (e.g., NetSuite, SAP, Intacct) and BI tools (e.g., Power BI, Tableau) to:

- Automate data pulls from GL, AP, and AR systems.

- Generate real-time dashboards for sponsors.

- Track covenant metrics dynamically.

For example, a cloud-based consolidation tool can reduce month-end close time by 30%, ensuring faster delivery to stakeholders. However, automation requires upfront investment in data governance - a messy chart of accounts or inconsistent cost centers will undermine even the best tools and is hard to recover from efficiently.

COMMON PITFALLS AND HOW TO AVOID THEM

Pitfall 1: Overloading Reports with Data

- Solution: Use appendices for granular data; keep main reports focused on insights.

Pitfall 2: Inconsistent Adjustments

- Solution: Document EBITDA add-back policies and apply them uniformly.

Pitfall 3: Late Submissions

- Solution: Implement a reporting calendar with buffer time for reviews.

Pitfall 4: Ignoring Non-Financial Metrics

- Solution: Integrate operational KPIs (e.g., customer churn, unit economics).

Pitfall 5: Underestimating Lender Queries

- Solution: Maintain a Q&A log from prior submissions to anticipate questions.

Mastering financial reporting for PE and lenders is a blend of technical rigor and strategic communication. By aligning reports with stakeholder priorities and leveraging technology, controllers can transform data into actionable intelligence—fueling both trust and growth.

CHAPTER 5:

ACCOUNTS PAYABLE AND RECEIVABLE MANAGEMENT

● ◆ ●

THE CRITICAL ROLE OF AP AND AR IN FINANCIAL CONTROLLERSHIP

Accounts Payable (AP) and Accounts Receivable (AR) are the lifeblood of any organization's cash flow. As a financial controller, mastering these functions ensures liquidity, operational efficiency, and strong vendor and customer relationships. AP involves managing outgoing payments to suppliers, while AR focuses on collecting revenue from customers. Both functions require meticulous attention to detail, robust internal controls, and strategic alignment with broader financial objectives. In private equity-owned companies, where cash flow optimization is paramount, AP and AR processes must be streamlined to meet investor expectations. A well-managed AP function ensures timely payments, avoids late fees, and maintains strong supplier relationships, while an efficient AR process accelerates cash inflows, reduces bad debt, and improves working capital.

The financial controller must oversee both functions to prevent bottlenecks that could disrupt operations or financial reporting. For example, delayed vendor payments can strain supplier relationships, leading to disrupted supply chains, while slow collections can create cash shortages, forcing reliance on expensive short-term financing. In private equity environments, where portfolio companies are often under pressure to maximize EBITDA and cash flow, AP and AR efficiency directly impacts valuation. Additionally, lenders scrutinize AR aging reports and AP turnover ratios when assessing creditworthiness, making these functions critical in debt covenant compliance.

Technology plays a pivotal role in modern AP and AR management. Automation tools, such as electronic invoicing, automated approval workflows, and AI-driven collections software, reduce manual errors and accelerate processing times. A controller must evaluate whether existing systems are scalable, particularly in high-growth or acquisition-driven environments. For instance, if a private equity firm acquires a new company, the controller must ensure seamless integration of AP and AR processes to avoid disruptions. Furthermore, regulatory compliance—such as sales tax remittance, 1099 reporting, and adherence to GAAP revenue recognition standards—must be embedded in these workflows to prevent costly penalties or audit findings.

> *Efficient AP and AR management isn't just about paying bills and collecting cash—it's about optimizing working capital to fuel growth and meet stakeholder expectations.*

Best Practices in Accounts Payable Management

A well-structured AP process begins with a clear invoice approval workflow. In private equity-backed firms, where cost discipline is critical, every payment must be justified and properly authorized. Implementing a three-way matching system—where purchase orders, receiving reports, and vendor invoices are cross-verified—reduces fraud risks and ensures accuracy. Controllers should enforce segregation of duties, ensuring that the employee approving payments is not the same person reconciling the bank account. This minimizes the risk of embezzlement and strengthens internal controls, a key concern for auditors and private equity sponsors alike.

Timely payments are essential, but so is optimizing payment terms. While some vendors demand net-30 terms, others may offer discounts for early payments (e.g., 2/10 net 30). A controller must weigh the cost of capital against potential savings—paying early to capture a 2% discount may be worthwhile if the company's cost of funds is lower. Conversely, stretching payables (without damaging relationships) can preserve cash, particularly in capital-intensive industries. In private equity, where portfolio companies often undergo restructuring, renegotiating vendor terms can unlock immediate working capital improvements.

Technology integration is crucial. AP automation platforms like Coupa, Stampli, Ramp, Bill.com, or SAP Ariba, amongst others, streamline invoice processing, reduce manual data errors, and provide real-time visibility into liabilities. These systems also facilitate electronic payments, reducing check fraud risks and processing costs. For multinational companies, managing cross-border payments adds complexity—foreign exchange risks, banking fees, and varying tax regulations must be carefully managed. Controllers should also monitor unclaimed property (escheatment) laws, as unprocessed vendor credits or uncashed checks can trigger compliance issues.

Fraud prevention is another critical AP responsibility. Common schemes include fictitious vendors, duplicate payments, and invoice padding. Implementing regular audits, vendor verification protocols, and anomaly detection tools can mitigate these risks. In private equity, where portfolio companies may undergo management changes, ensuring AP controls survive leadership transitions is vital. Finally, the controller must ensure AP data flows accurately into the general ledger, supporting month-end close and financial reporting. Discrepancies in accrued liabilities can distort financial statements, leading to misinformed decisions by private equity sponsors or lenders.

- Implement a three-way matching system for invoices
- Enforce segregation of duties in payment approvals
- Leverage early payment discounts where financially beneficial
- Automate AP workflows to reduce manual errors
- Conduct regular fraud risk assessments

Optimizing Accounts Receivable for Cash Flow Efficiency

Accounts Receivable management is equally critical, as it directly impacts liquidity and working capital. The financial controller must ensure that billing is accurate, timely, and aligned with contractual terms. In private equity-owned companies, where cash flow is closely monitored, delays in AR collections can trigger liquidity crises or covenant breaches. The first step in AR optimization is establishing clear credit policies. Before extending credit, customers should undergo credit checks, and terms (e.g., net-30, net-60) should be set based on risk assessments. High-risk clients may require upfront payments or letters of credit.

Invoicing accuracy is paramount. Errors in billing—such as incorrect pricing, missing purchase orders, or misapplied payments—delay collections and strain customer relationships. Automated billing systems reduce manual entry errors and can integrate with CRM or ERP platforms to ensure consistency. For recurring revenue models (e.g., SaaS companies), subscription billing tools automate invoicing and dunning processes. Controllers should also monitor billing disputes closely, as unresolved issues can lead to write-offs. In private equity, where EBITDA margins are scrutinized, minimizing bad debt is essential.

Collections management requires a structured approach. Aging reports should be reviewed weekly, with escalating follow-ups—emails, calls, and, if necessary, third-party collections. Offering multiple payment options (ACH, credit cards, online portals) accelerates cash inflows. For large or strategic customers, the controller may negotiate payment plans rather than risking defaults. In distressed situations, factoring or receivable financing can provide liquidity, though at a cost. Private equity sponsors often push for aggressive AR management, as improved Days Sales Outstanding (DSO) directly enhances cash flow and valuation multiples.

Revenue recognition compliance is another layer of complexity. Under GAAP (ASC 606), revenue must be recognized when performance obligations are satisfied, which may not align with cash receipts. Controllers must ensure AR systems accurately track deferred revenue, unbilled receivables, and contract liabilities. This is particularly relevant in industries with long-term contracts (e.g., construction, software). Misclassification can lead to financial restatements, eroding investor confidence. Finally, AR data must seamlessly integrate into financial reporting, providing private equity sponsors with real-time visibility into cash flow trends.

- Establish and enforce customer credit policies

- Automate invoicing to minimize errors

- Implement a proactive collections escalation process

- Ensure GAAP-compliant revenue recognition

- Regularly reconcile AR subledger to the general ledger

THE INTERSECTION OF AP, AR, AND TREASURY MANAGEMENT

AP and AR do not operate in isolation—they are deeply interconnected with treasury management. The financial controller must align both functions with cash flow forecasting to ensure liquidity. For example, if AR collections are delayed, the controller may need to adjust AP payments or arrange short-term financing to cover obligations. In private equity, where portfolio companies often carry significant debt, mismanaging this balance can lead to covenant violations or liquidity shortfalls.

Cash flow forecasting relies on accurate AP and AR data. The controller should maintain rolling 13-week cash flow projections, incorporating expected vendor payments, customer receipts, and seasonal fluctuations. Scenario analysis—such as modeling the impact of a major customer default or a supply chain disruption—helps mitigate risks. Private equity sponsors often demand granular cash flow reporting, as it directly impacts dividend distributions and exit strategies.

Working capital optimization is another key focus. Techniques like dynamic discounting (where suppliers are paid early in exchange for discounts) or supply chain financing (where a third-party financier pays suppliers early) can improve margins. On the AR side, securitization or factoring monetizes receivables, though at a cost. The controller must evaluate these tools' ROI, ensuring they align with the company's cost of capital and strategic goals.

Bank relationship management is also critical. AP and AR processes often depend on banking infrastructure—lockboxes for AR, ACH/wire platforms for AP. The controller should negotiate favorable banking terms, such as reduced transaction fees or improved fraud protection. In multinational settings, multi-currency accounts and hedging strategies may be necessary to mitigate FX risks.

> *Treasury isn't just about managing money—it's about orchestrating AP, AR, and financing to keep the business agile and solvent.*

TECHNOLOGY AND FUTURE TRENDS IN AP/AR MANAGEMENT

The future of AP and AR lies in automation, AI, and blockchain. Robotic Process Automation can handle repetitive tasks like invoice data entry or payment reconciliations, freeing staff for other duties. AI-driven tools predict payment delays, flag high-risk customers, or optimize payment timing. Blockchain-enabled smart contracts could eventually automate invoice approvals and settlements, reducing fraud and delays.

For private equity-owned firms, investing in modern AP/AR systems pays dividends at exit. Buyers scrutinize the quality of financial operations, and streamlined processes enhance valuation. Controllers must stay ahead of trends, ensuring their systems scale with growth and M&A activity.

In conclusion, AP and AR are not and should not be perceived as back-office afterthoughts—they are strategic levers for financial controllers. Mastering them ensures liquidity, compliance, and value creation in private equity environments.

CHAPTER 6:

PAYROLL AND EMPLOYEE COMPENSATION

● ◆ ●

THE CRITICAL ROLE OF PAYROLL IN FINANCIAL CONTROLLERSHIP

Payroll is one of the most critical functions within any organization, directly impacting employee satisfaction, regulatory compliance, and financial accuracy. As a financial controller, overseeing payroll means ensuring that employees are paid accurately and on time while maintaining strict adherence to tax laws, labor regulations, and internal controls. A single payroll error can lead to employee dissatisfaction, regulatory penalties, or even legal disputes, making this function a high-stakes responsibility. Unlike other accounting functions, payroll is highly visible to all employees, meaning mistakes are quickly noticed and can damage morale and trust in the finance department. Additionally, payroll is often one of the largest expenses for a company, particularly in labor-intensive industries, making it a key area for cost control and financial forecasting.

Private equity-owned companies often have additional complexities in payroll management, including equity-based compensation, performance bonuses, and deferred compensation structures that must be accurately tracked and reported. These elements require meticulous record-keeping to ensure compliance with both GAAP and tax regulations. Furthermore, payroll data feeds into multiple financial reports, including the income statement (as salaries and wages expense), the balance sheet (accrued payroll liabilities), and cash flow statements (cash outflows for payroll disbursements). Given these interdependencies, the financial controller must ensure seamless integration between payroll systems and the general ledger to maintain accurate financial reporting.

Another layer of complexity arises when dealing with multi-state or international payroll, where varying tax jurisdictions impose different withholding requirements, labor laws, and reporting obligations. For example, some states have unique paid leave laws, while others mandate different overtime calculations. International payroll introduces additional challenges, such as foreign currency exchange, expatriate tax considerations, and compliance with local labor regulations. A financial controller must work closely with HR and legal teams to ensure payroll policies align with all applicable laws while minimizing tax exposure.

Given the high volume of transactions and the sensitivity of payroll data, strong internal controls are essential. Segregation of duties, approval workflows, and periodic reconciliations between payroll registers and bank statements help prevent fraud and errors. Automated payroll software can reduce manual intervention, but controllers must still validate system outputs and ensure proper access controls are in place. Regular audits—both internal and external—should review payroll processes to identify weaknesses and ensure compliance with company policies and regulatory requirements.

> *Payroll is not just about cutting checks—it's about ensuring compliance, maintaining trust, and optimizing financial performance.*

KEY PAYROLL PROCESSES AND BEST PRACTICES

Payroll Processing and Disbursement

Processing payroll involves multiple steps, from collecting time and attendance data to calculating gross pay, withholding taxes, and issuing payments. The financial controller must ensure that all inputs—such as hours worked, overtime, bonuses, and deductions—are accurately captured before payroll is processed. Automated time-tracking systems can reduce errors, but manual reviews are still necessary to verify exceptions, such as unpaid leave or shift differentials. Once gross pay is calculated, payroll teams must apply federal, state, and local tax withholdings, as well as voluntary deductions (e.g., retirement contributions, health insurance premiums).

Disbursement methods vary, with direct deposit being the most common, though some employees may prefer paper checks or paycards. Controllers must ensure that payroll funds are transferred to the correct bank accounts and that unclaimed wages are properly escheated to state authorities if necessary. Reconciliation between payroll registers, bank statements and the general ledger is crucial to confirm that all payments were processed correctly. Any discrepancies must be investigated immediately to prevent fraud or compliance issues. DO not wait until the audit is upon you to have the payroll reconciliations done, as it can be a significant project, open to surprises, at the most difficult time of year for the accounting team.

For private equity-owned companies, payroll may also include special compensation arrangements, such as profit-sharing, stock options, or retention bonuses tied to acquisition milestones. These require additional tracking to ensure proper accounting under GAAP and tax reporting. Controllers must also monitor payroll-related liabilities, such as accrued bonuses, paid time off (PTO) balances, and payroll tax deposits, to ensure they are accurately reflected in financial statements.

Tax Compliance and Reporting

Payroll taxes are among the most heavily regulated areas of finance, with strict filing deadlines and penalties for non-compliance. Financial controllers must ensure accurate withholding of federal income tax, Social Security, Medicare, and applicable state/local taxes. Employers are also responsible for paying their share of payroll taxes, including Federal Unemployment Tax (FUTA) and State Unemployment Tax (SUTA). Quarterly filings (Form 941 in the U.S.) and annual reconciliations (Form W-2 for employees and Form 1099 for contractors) must be completed accurately and on time.

International payroll adds another layer of complexity, as tax treaties, social security agreements, and local reporting requirements vary by country. Controllers may need to work with global payroll providers or in-country experts to ensure compliance. Transfer pricing considerations may also arise if employees work across borders, requiring careful documentation to avoid tax disputes.

Employee Benefits and Retirement Plans

Beyond base salaries, employee compensation often involves benefits such as health insurance, retirement plans, and stock-based compensation. Controllers must ensure that these benefits are accurately recorded in payroll systems and properly expensed in financial statements. For example, employer contributions to 401(k) plans must be matched correctly and reported in compliance with ERISA regulations. Stock options and restricted stock units (RSUs) require fair value accounting under ASC 718, with expenses recognized over the vesting period.

Health and welfare benefits, including medical, dental, and disability insurance, must also be tracked for both payroll deductions and employer-paid portions. Self-insured plans may require additional actuarial valuations to estimate liabilities. Controllers should work closely with HR to ensure that benefit enrollments, terminations, and changes are promptly reflected in payroll systems to avoid over- or under-withholding.

Payroll Audits and Internal Controls

Regular payroll audits are essential to detect errors, prevent fraud, and ensure compliance. Key controls include:

- Segregation of duties between payroll processing, approval, and disbursement

- Periodic reconciliations of payroll registers to general ledger accounts (monthly is best practice)

- Review of unusual payroll transactions (e.g., excessive overtime, duplicate payments)

- Verification of new and terminated employees to prevent "ghost" payroll fraud

- Monitoring of payroll tax filings and deposits to avoid penalties

Internal audits should also assess whether payroll systems are properly configured to enforce company policies, such as overtime rules and paid time off accruals. Any weaknesses identified should be addressed through process improvements or additional controls.

Payroll in Mergers, Acquisitions, and Divestitures

During M&A transactions, payroll integration (or separation) is a critical task. Acquiring companies must harmonize payroll systems, policies, and employee classifications to ensure consistency. Due diligence should review target company practices for compliance risks, such as misclassification of employees vs. independent contractors or unpaid payroll taxes. Post-acquisition, controllers must oversee the transition of payroll data, ensuring that employee records, tax withholdings, and benefit enrollments are accurately transferred.

Divestitures require careful planning to ensure that payroll responsibilities are clearly delineated between the seller and buyer. Employee transitions must be managed to avoid gaps in pay or benefits, and final payroll reconciliations should confirm that all liabilities (e.g., accrued PTO, bonuses) are properly settled.

KEY POINTS

Payroll is a foundational function that demands precision, compliance, and strategic oversight. Financial controllers must balance operational efficiency with regulatory adherence, ensuring that employees are paid accurately while safeguarding the company from financial and legal risks. By implementing strong controls, leveraging technology, and staying informed on evolving labor and tax laws, controllers can turn payroll from a routine task into a strategic asset that supports organizational success.

CHAPTER 7:

TREASURY MANAGEMENT AND CASH FLOW FORECASTING

● ◆ ●

THE CRITICAL ROLE OF TREASURY MANAGEMENT IN PRIVATE EQUITY

Treasury management is the lifeblood of any private equity-backed company, ensuring liquidity, optimizing working capital, and safeguarding financial stability. Unlike founder-owned or venture capital-backed firms, PE portfolio companies operate under heightened scrutiny from sponsors who demand rigorous cash flow discipline to meet debt obligations and drive returns. The financial controller plays a pivotal role in designing and executing treasury strategies that align with the company's growth objectives while mitigating risks.

Private equity ownership introduces unique challenges, such as leveraged capital structures with tight covenants, aggressive growth targets, and frequent M&A activity. These factors amplify the need for precise cash flow visibility. Unlike VC-backed startups—where cash burn is often tolerated for rapid scaling—or founder-led businesses—

where cash reserves may be less formalized—PE firms prioritize cash efficiency. Controllers must balance short-term operational needs (e.g., payroll, vendor payments) with long-term strategic goals (e.g., debt repayment, capex funding).

A robust treasury function begins with cash positioning, the daily tracking of cash inflows and outflows across all accounts. Controllers must consolidate data from disparate systems (e.g., ERPs, bank portals) to create a real-time view of liquidity. This is especially critical in PE, where unexpected cash shortfalls can trigger covenant breaches. For example, a manufacturing portfolio company might use cash sweeps to centralize funds from regional subsidiaries, ensuring idle cash is deployed effectively.

In private equity, cash is king—but visibility is queen. You can't manage what you can't measure.

Key responsibilities include:

- Daily cash reconciliation
- Monitoring debt compliance (e.g., debt service coverage ratios, leverage ratios)
- Optimizing interest expense via debt structuring
- Managing banking relationships and credit facilities

CASH FLOW FORECASTING: FROM SHORT-TERM LIQUIDITY TO LONG-TERM PLANNING

Cash flow forecasting is the cornerstone of financial controllership in PE-backed companies. Unlike static budgets, forecasts are dynamic tools that adapt to operational changes, market shifts, and M&A activity. Controllers must develop 13-week cash flow models for near-term liquidity management and long-term (12–24 month) projections to align with sponsor exit timelines.

Short-term forecasts focus on operational cycle components:

- Accounts Receivable: Tracking collections and DSO (Days Sales Outstanding) trends. For instance, a SaaS company might model cash inflows based on subscription renewal dates.

- Accounts Payable: Timing vendor payments to preserve cash without damaging relationships.

- Payroll and Taxes: Accounting for biweekly payroll cycles and quarterly tax estimates.

Long-term forecasts integrate strategic initiatives, such as capex projects or acquisitions. A controller at a PE-owned healthcare provider, for example, might model the cash impact of a new clinic rollout, including upfront construction expenses and delayed revenue recognition. Sensitivity analysis is critical as PE sponsors often demand "base case," "upside," and "downside" scenarios to assess risk.

Common pitfalls include over-reliance on historical trends (which may not reflect post-acquisition synergies) and underestimating working capital swings. A best practice is to collaborate with department heads (e.g., sales, procurement) to validate assumptions.

DEBT COMPLIANCE AND COVENANT MANAGEMENT

PE portfolio companies typically carry significant debt, often structured with complex covenants (e.g., minimum EBITDA thresholds, leverage ratios). The controller must ensure compliance while maximizing financial flexibility.

Key steps:

- Covenant Tracking: Automate calculations (e.g., debt/EBITDA) within financial systems to avoid manual errors.

- Communication with Lenders: Proactively disclose potential breaches and negotiate waivers if needed.

- Scenario Planning: Model the impact of operational setbacks (e.g., a customer bankruptcy) on covenant metrics.

For example, a retail chain acquired by a PE firm might face a liquidity crunch during seasonal inventory buildup. The controller could assist in arranging a temporary revolver drawdown or negotiate a covenant holiday with lenders.

WORKING CAPITAL OPTIMIZATION

Reducing working capital drag is a high-leverage activity in PE. Techniques include:

- Inventory Management: Implementing just-in-time (JIT) systems to free up cash.

- Receivables Acceleration: Offering early-payment discounts or factoring receivables.

- Payables Discipline: Extending payment terms strategically (e.g., from 30 to 45 days).

TECHNOLOGY AND AUTOMATION IN TREASURY

Modern treasury relies on tools like:

- TMS (Treasury Management Systems): Automate cash pooling, FX hedging, and reporting.

- AP/AR Automation: Reduce manual processing and errors.

- Blockchain: Emerging use cases for intercompany settlements.

Controllers should advocate for tech investments that enhance cash visibility—a $100k software spend can save millions in reduced borrowing costs. Use foresight when when choosing a solution, as you do not want to realize too late the selection is insufficient for the longer term.

KEY POINTS

In PE-backed environments, treasury isn't just about survival—it's about fueling growth while keeping sponsors and lenders confident. Mastery of cash flow forecasting and working capital levers separates good controllers from indispensable ones.

CHAPTER 8:

BUDGETING AND FORECASTING FOR GROWTH

• ◆ •

THE STRATEGIC ROLE OF BUDGETING AND FORECASTING IN PRIVATE EQUITY

Budgeting and forecasting are not merely administrative tasks—they are the financial backbone of any private equity backed company. Unlike traditional founder-owned businesses, where budgets may be more flexible and growth targets less aggressive, PE-owned companies operate under strict performance expectations tied to investor returns. As a financial controller, your role in budgeting and forecasting is pivotal because these processes directly influence operational decisions, capital allocation, and exit strategies. A well-structured budget serves as a roadmap, while accurate forecasts act as a reality check against market conditions and internal performance. Private equity sponsors demand precision, accountability, and agility in financial planning, meaning controllers must balance detailed historical data with forward-looking assumptions.

One of the key differences between PE-owned companies and venture capital backed or founder-led businesses is the emphasis on value creation within a defined timeframe.

While VCs may tolerate longer growth horizons in exchange for disruptive innovation, PE firms typically operate on 3-7 year investment cycles, requiring aggressive yet achievable financial targets. Founder-owned businesses, on the other hand, may prioritize sustainability over rapid scaling, making their budgeting processes less rigid. For controllers, this means PE budgets must incorporate not just operational efficiency but also strategic initiatives like cost optimization, revenue expansion, and EBITDA growth.

> *"A budget is telling your money where to go instead of wondering where it went." — Dave Ramsey*

To align with PE expectations, controllers must ensure budgets are:

- Tied to key performance indicators (KPIs) such as revenue growth, gross margin, and working capital efficiency

- Built with input from cross-functional leaders (sales, operations, HR) to ensure feasibility

- Flexible enough to adapt to market shifts but disciplined enough to prevent overspending

- Integrated with rolling forecasts to allow mid-course corrections

- Transparently reported to stakeholders with variance analysis

BUILDING A HIGH-PERFORMANCE BUDGET

Step 1: Establishing the Baseline

Before projecting future performance, controllers must thoroughly analyze historical financial data. This includes reviewing past income statements, balance sheets, and cash flow statements to identify trends, seasonality, and anomalies. For PE-owned companies, historical data should be adjusted for one-time events, discontinued operations, or non-recurring expenses to ensure a clean baseline. If the company has undergone recent acquisitions or divestitures, pro forma financials must be incorporated to reflect the new operational structure.

Step 2: Setting Realistic Revenue Targets

Revenue forecasting is often the most challenging yet critical component of budgeting. Unlike founder-led businesses, where growth may be organic, PE-backed firms frequently pursue aggressive top-line expansion through both organic and inorganic means (e.g., M&A, market penetration). Controllers must work closely with sales and marketing teams to validate assumptions around customer acquisition costs, pricing strategies, and market demand. Scenario analysis—best-case, base-case, and worst-case—should be conducted to stress-test revenue projections.

Step 3: Cost Structure Optimization

PE firms scrutinize cost structures to maximize EBITDA. Controllers must ensure budgets account for both fixed and variable costs while identifying areas for efficiency. This includes:

- Labor costs (salaries, benefits, contractor expenses)
- Supply chain and procurement efficiencies
- Overhead reduction opportunities
- Capital expenditure (CapEx) planning
- Compliance and regulatory cost buffers

Step 4: Cash Flow Integration

A budget without cash flow alignment is a recipe for liquidity crises. Controllers must ensure that revenue and expense projections translate into realistic cash flow forecasts, accounting for timing differences in receivables, payables, and debt servicing. PE sponsors often require weekly or bi-weekly cash flow updates, making this a high-priority deliverable.

Step 5: Stakeholder Alignment and Approval

Once the budget is drafted, controllers must present it to senior management and the PE sponsors, justifying assumptions and demonstrating alignment with strategic goals. Any discrepancies between operational leaders and financial projections must be resolved before finalization.

ROLLING FORECASTS: THE AGILE ALTERNATIVE TO STATIC BUDGETS

Why PE Firms Prefer Rolling Forecasts

Unlike traditional annual budgets, rolling forecasts provide continuous updates, typically on a quarterly or monthly basis. This approach is particularly valuable in PE environments where market conditions and operational performance can shift rapidly. Rolling forecasts allow controllers to:

- Adjust for macroeconomic changes (e.g., inflation, interest rates)

- Incorporate actual performance data in real-time

- Reallocate resources dynamically to high-growth areas

- Provide PE sponsors with up-to-date visibility into financial health

Implementing Rolling Forecasts Effectively

To transition from static budgets to rolling forecasts, controllers must:

- Leverage Financial Systems: Use ERP and FP&A software to automate data collection and reporting.

- Establish Clear Timelines: Define update frequencies (e.g., quarterly re-forecasts) and responsibilities.

- Maintain Historical Comparisons: Ensure new forecasts are benchmarked against prior projections to track accuracy.

- Communicate Changes Proactively: Keep leadership and PE sponsors informed of material adjustments.

VARIANCE ANALYSIS: BRIDGING THE GAP BETWEEN PLAN AND REALITY

Identifying and Explaining Variances

Variance analysis is the process of comparing actual financial results to budgeted or forecasted figures. For PE-owned companies, this is not just an exercise in accountability but a tool for course correction. Controllers must categorize variances as:

- Revenue Variances: Driven by pricing, volume, or market conditions

- Cost Variances: Due to inefficiencies, inflation, or unplanned expenses

- Cash Flow Variances: Resulting from timing delays or collections issues

Actionable Reporting for PE Sponsors

- PE firms expect concise yet insightful variance reports that highlight:

- Material deviations (e.g., >5% variance)

- Root causes and corrective actions

- Impact on annual targets and EBITDA

- Revised forecasts if necessary

BEST PRACTICES FOR CONTROLLERS IN PE-BACKED COMPANIES

Collaboration with Operational Teams

Controllers cannot work in isolation. Effective budgeting and forecasting require deep collaboration with departments like sales, operations, and HR to ensure assumptions are grounded in reality.

Leveraging Technology

Modern FP&A tools (e.g., Adaptive Insights, Anaplan) can automate data aggregation, scenario modeling, and reporting, freeing controllers to focus on strategic analysis.

Maintaining Flexibility Without Sacrificing Discipline

While agility is crucial, controllers must ensure that frequent forecast updates do not lead to a lack of accountability. Clear governance around budget adjustments is essential and detailed documentation retained.

Continuous Improvement

Post-mortem reviews of budgeting accuracy and forecast reliability should be conducted annually to refine processes and improve future projections.

By mastering these principles, financial controllers can drive value creation in PE-backed companies, ensuring that budgets and forecasts are not just compliance exercises but strategic tools for growth.

CHAPTER 9:

INTERNAL CONTROLS AND FRAUD PREVENTION

● ◆ ●

THE CRITICAL ROLE OF INTERNAL CONTROLS

Internal controls are the backbone of financial integrity within any organization, but they take on heightened importance in private equity owned portfolio companies where stakeholders demand transparency, accuracy, and accountability. As a financial controller, your role is to design, implement, and monitor these controls to safeguard assets, ensure compliance with GAAP, and mitigate risks of fraud or misstatement. Unlike founder-owned businesses, where processes may be informal, PE-backed firms require rigorous controls to meet investor expectations and lender covenants. Venture capital backed firms, while also investor driven, often prioritize growth over control maturity—until a liquidity event necessitates tighter governance. The distinction lies in the level of scrutiny: PE firms enforce structured oversight from day one, while VCs may tolerate looser controls until scaling demands them.

A well-structured internal control framework aligns with the COSO (Committee of Sponsoring Organizations) model, which emphasizes five components: control environment, risk assessment, control activities, information/communication, and monitoring. For example, segregating duties between accounts payable and receivable clerks prevents a single employee from both authorizing payments and recording them—a classic fraud risk. Similarly, requiring dual approvals for expenditures above a threshold (e.g., $10,000) adds a layer of oversight. These controls aren't just about compliance; they directly impact valuation. During due diligence for an exit, weak controls can lead to price adjustments or even deal collapse.

> *Fraud thrives in the absence of controls. A controller's job isn't just to detect it but to design systems that make it nearly impossible.*

Consider the case of a mid-market manufacturing company that failed to reconcile inventory counts to financial records for six months. By the time the discrepancy was caught, $2M in stolen goods had been written off as "shrinkage." The root cause? Lack of physical inventory audits and over-reliance on a single warehouse manager. PE sponsors replaced the entire finance team post-acquisition.

KEY QUESTIONS TO ASK WHEN EVALUATING CONTROLS:

- Are roles segregated to prevent conflicts of interest?

- Are all transactions documented and reviewed by independent parties?

- Is access to financial systems restricted based on job function?

- Are anomalies investigated promptly, with corrective actions tracked?

- Are controls tested annually for effectiveness?

COMMON FRAUD RISKS AND RED FLAGS

Fraud manifests in three primary forms: asset misappropriation (e.g., theft), financial statement fraud (e.g., revenue inflation), and corruption (e.g., bribery). In PE-owned companies, the pressure to hit EBITDA targets can inadvertently incentivize manipulation, such as delaying expense recognition or prematurely booking sales. Controllers must balance operational agility with skepticism, especially when management pushes for aggressive accounting interpretations. A classic red flag is a department head who refuses to take vacation—a tactic often used to hide ongoing schemes.

Accounts payable is a frequent fraud hotspot. Phantom vendors, duplicate payments, and inflated invoices can slip through if controls are weak. For instance, a construction company's AP clerk created a shell vendor with a name nearly identical to a legitimate contractor, diverting $500K over two years. The fraud was uncovered only when a bank reconciliation revealed inconsistent check endorsements. Implementing vendor verification (e.g., W-9 validation) and three-way matching (PO, receipt, invoice) could have prevented this.

In accounts receivable, "lapping" is a pervasive threat— where an employee applies payments from one customer to another's account to conceal theft. Regular AR aging reviews and customer confirmation audits are critical deterrents. One PE-backed SaaS company discovered a collections specialist had been lapping payments for months, masking $300K in stolen cash. The fix? Automating payment applications and requiring supervisory review of write-offs.

Payroll fraud, though less discussed, is equally damaging. "Ghost employees" (fictitious workers on payroll) or inflated hours can bleed thousands monthly. A retail chain's HR manager added a relative to payroll who never worked a shift, siphoning $150K before an anonymous tip exposed it. Solutions include biometric time clocks, periodic payroll audits, and cross-checking employee lists against HR records.

> *The best fraud prevention isn't a policy—it's a culture. Employees who see leadership prioritize ethics won't game the system.*

DESIGNING EFFECTIVE CONTROL FRAMEWORKS

Start with a risk assessment to identify vulnerabilities unique to your industry and organizational structure. A healthcare provider's risks (e.g., Medicare billing fraud) differ from a logistics firm's (e.g., fuel skimming). Map out processes end-to-end, from procurement to financial reporting, and pinpoint where controls are missing or inadequate. For example, if employees can override system-generated journal entries without approval, that's a gap needing remediation.

Segregation of duties is non-negotiable. No single individual should control all aspects of a transaction—authorization, recording, custody, and reconciliation must be split. In smaller teams, this can be challenging, but compensating controls (e.g., periodic management reviews) can fill gaps. A PE-backed tech startup learned this the hard way when its CFO, who also handled cash disbursements, embezzled $1.2M by forging signatures. Post-incident, the company implemented mandatory dual signatures for wire transfers and outsourced treasury functions.

Automation reduces human error and fraud opportunities. Tools like BlackLine and Floqast for reconciliations or Coupa (among other solutions) for procure-to-pay workflows enforce policy adherence. One industrial manufacturer cut invoice fraud by 80% after deploying AI to flag duplicate or anomalous payments. However, technology isn't a silver bullet—override capabilities and admin access must be tightly controlled.

Documentation is your defense. Maintain clear policies (e.g., "All journal entries over $50K require CFO approval") and train staff annually. During an audit, regulators will scrutinize not just whether controls exist, but whether they're consistently followed.

- Conduct a quarterly risk assessment to update controls for new threats.

- Automate high-risk processes (e.g., payment approvals, reconciliations).

- Rotate duties among staff to prevent complacency.

- Require mandatory vacations for finance personnel.

- Partner with internal audit or third-party firms for unbiased reviews.

MONITORING AND CONTINUOUS IMPROVEMENT

Controls degrade over time if not actively monitored. Implement key performance indicators to measure effectiveness, such as "percentage of invoices paid without three-way matching" or "average time to close month-end reconciliations."

Surprise audits are a potent deterrent. Randomly selecting a month's transactions for deep-dive testing keeps teams vigilant. A consumer goods company discovered a warehouse supervisor stealing inventory by conducting unannounced cycle counts—fraudsters rarely expect checks outside the annual audit.

Whistleblower programs, mandated by the Dodd-Frank Act for public companies, are equally valuable for PE portfolio firms. Ensure reports are investigated by an independent party (e.g., outside counsel) to avoid retaliation claims.

Post-mortems after control failures are vital learning opportunities. When a software company's payroll system was hacked due to weak password protocols, they not only fixed the IT controls but also ran phishing tests to train employees. PE sponsors often require "lessons learned" reports after incidents to prevent recurrence.

A control framework is like a muscle—it weakens without exercise. Test it, stress it, and adapt it.

THE PRIVATE EQUITY LENS: CONTROLS AS VALUE DRIVERS

PE firms view robust controls as both risk mitigation and value creation. At acquisition, they'll scrutinize control gaps that could affect valuation (e.g., unreconciled intercompany accounts). Post-close, they expect controllers to standardize processes across portfolio companies to streamline reporting and reduce "noise" in financials. Some PE sponsors mandate all portfolio companies use the same ERP system, enabling centralized monitoring of anomalies.

During exits, buyers (especially strategic acquirers) will dissect control histories. A clean audit trail and documented compliance with SOX-like standards can justify premium pricing. Conversely, a history of material weaknesses may trigger indemnity holds.

For controllers, the message is clear: Internal controls aren't just about ticking boxes—they're strategic tools that protect and enhance enterprise value. In the high-stakes world of private equity, that's a language every sponsor understands.

CHAPTER 10:

ACCOUNTING POLICIES AND PROCEDURES

● ◆ ●

THE FOUNDATION OF FINANCIAL INTEGRITY

Accounting policies and procedures serve as the backbone of any well-functioning finance department. They provide the framework for consistency, accuracy, and compliance in financial reporting, ensuring that all transactions are recorded uniformly and in accordance with Generally Accepted Accounting Principles. Without standardized policies, financial statements can become unreliable, leading to misinformed decision-making, regulatory scrutiny, and even financial penalties. For private equity-owned companies, where transparency and efficiency are paramount, having robust accounting policies is not just a best practice—it's a necessity. These policies must be documented, communicated, and enforced across all levels of the organization to mitigate risks and maintain investor confidence.

A well-structured accounting policy manual should cover every critical financial process, from revenue recognition to expense allocation, and should be reviewed annually to reflect changes in regulations, business operations, or ownership structures. For example, if a company expands internationally, its policies must address foreign currency translation, transfer pricing, and tax compliance in new jurisdictions. Similarly, if a private equity firm acquires a new portfolio company, the controller must ensure that the target's accounting practices align with the parent company's policies to facilitate smooth consolidation. The manual should also define roles and responsibilities, specifying who approves journal entries, reconciliations, and financial reports to prevent unauthorized adjustments.

> *Clear accounting policies are the guardrails that keep a company's financial reporting on track. Without them, even the most skilled finance team can veer into inconsistency and error.*

One of the most common pitfalls in accounting policy development is creating overly complex documents that are difficult to implement. Policies should be detailed enough to provide guidance but flexible enough to accommodate reasonable judgment calls. For instance, while GAAP provides broad principles for revenue recognition, a company's policy must specify how it applies those principles to its unique business model—whether it recognizes revenue at the point of sale, upon delivery, or over time for subscription services. Another critical consideration is the balance between automation and manual controls. While accounting software can enforce policy compliance through system rules, human oversight remains essential for reviewing exceptions and ensuring that automated processes function as intended.

In private equity environment, where portfolio companies often undergo rapid growth or restructuring, accounting policies must be scalable. A policy that works for a $50 million company may not suffice when the business grows to $500 million. Controllers should anticipate these changes and draft policies with scalability in mind, ensuring that processes like month-end close, intercompany eliminations, and management reporting can handle increased transaction volumes without sacrificing accuracy. Additionally, policies should be aligned with the expectations of private equity sponsors, who often demand granular financial data and real-time visibility into performance metrics. This means incorporating key performance indicators, cash flow benchmarks, and EBITDA adjustments into the policy framework.

Finally, training and enforcement are just as important as the policies themselves. A policy is only effective if employees understand and follow it. Regular training sessions, supplemented by quick-reference guides and checklists, can help embed these standards into daily operations. For example, a billing clerk should know exactly when and how to record accounts receivable, while a staff accountant should understand the thresholds for capitalizing versus expensing an asset. Internal audits can then verify compliance, identifying gaps where additional training or policy refinements may be needed.

Key Components of an Accounting Policy Manual

An effective accounting policy manual is comprehensive yet concise, covering all critical areas while avoiding unnecessary complexity. Below are the essential components that every controller should include:

Revenue Recognition

Revenue recognition policies must align with GAAP (or IFRS, if applicable) and reflect the company's specific business model. For SaaS companies, this might involve deferred revenue schedules, while manufacturers may need policies for recognizing revenue upon transfer of control. The policy should specify:

- Criteria for determining when revenue is earned

- Treatment of discounts, rebates, and returns

- Handling of multi-element arrangements (e.g., bundled products and services)

- Procedures for estimating variable consideration (e.g., bonuses or penalties)

- Documentation requirements for supporting revenue entries

Expense Classification and Capitalization

Clear guidelines on expense categorization prevent misclassification, which can distort financial statements and tax filings. Policies should define:

- Thresholds for capitalizing fixed assets versus expensing repairs

- Amortization schedules for intangible assets

- Treatment of prepaid expenses and accruals

- Procedures for allocating shared costs (e.g., overhead)

- Approval workflows for capital expenditures

Internal Controls and Fraud Prevention

Strong internal controls are non-negotiable, especially in private equity-owned companies where stakeholders demand accountability. Policies should outline:

- Segregation of duties for authorization, recording, and reconciliation

- Approval hierarchies for expenditures and journal entries

- Regular reconciliation schedules for high-risk accounts (e.g., cash, receivables)

- Whistleblower protocols for reporting suspicious activity

- Periodic internal audit procedures

Month-End and Year-End Close Processes

A structured close process ensures timely and accurate financial reporting. Policies should detail:

- Deadlines for preliminary and final closes

- Required reconciliations and supporting documentation

- Roles of corporate accounting vs. business unit teams

- Procedures for adjusting entries and error correction

- Communication protocols with auditors

Compliance with Tax and Regulatory Requirements

Tax policies must address federal, state, and local obligations, including:

- Sales tax collection and remittance procedures

- Transfer pricing documentation for intercompany transactions

- Estimated tax payment schedules

- Policies for recognizing tax contingencies

- Coordination with external tax advisors

IMPLEMENTING AND ENFORCING POLICIES

Creating policies is only the first step; ensuring adherence requires a structured implementation plan. Controllers should:

- Communicate Clearly: Distribute the policy manual to all relevant employees and hold training sessions to explain key provisions.

- Integrate with Systems: Configure accounting software to enforce policy rules (e.g., auto-flagging uncoded expenses).

- Monitor Compliance: Use internal audits to identify deviations and address them promptly.

- Update Regularly: Revisit policies annually or when significant changes occur (e.g., new GAAP standards, M&A activity).

THE ROLE OF TECHNOLOGY IN POLICY ADHERENCE

Modern accounting systems can automate policy enforcement, reducing human error. Features like:

- Workflow Automation: Routing approvals based on predefined rules.

- Audit Trails: Tracking all financial transactions for transparency.

- Real-Time Reporting: Flagging anomalies as they occur.

KEY POINTS

Accounting policies and procedures are the foundation of financial integrity. By developing, implementing, and enforcing clear guidelines, controllers can ensure accuracy, compliance, and investor confidence in private equity-owned companies.

CHAPTER 11:

TAX COMPLIANCE AND STRATEGY

● ◆ ●

TAX COMPLIANCE

Tax compliance is one of the most critical yet complex responsibilities of a financial controller. Unlike other accounting functions, tax obligations are governed by a labyrinth of federal, state, local, and international regulations that require meticulous attention to detail, proactive planning, and strategic foresight. A controller must ensure that the company remains compliant while optimizing tax liabilities—balancing risk mitigation with financial efficiency. This chapter explores the multifaceted world of tax compliance, from foundational obligations like sales tax and payroll tax to advanced considerations such as transfer pricing and international tax structuring. Whether you're working in a private equity-backed firm, a venture capital-funded startup, or a founder-owned business, understanding these tax dynamics is essential for safeguarding the company's financial health and supporting its growth trajectory.

UNDERSTANDING THE TAX LANDSCAPE

Tax obligations vary significantly depending on the ownership structure of a company—private equity, venture capital, or founder-owned. Private equity-owned companies often face heightened scrutiny due to leveraged buyouts, complex holding structures, and aggressive growth targets, which can trigger unique tax implications. Venture capital-backed firms, on the other hand, may prioritize tax credits (such as R&D credits) and loss carryforwards to offset early-stage losses. Founder-owned businesses typically have simpler structures but may struggle with succession planning and estate tax considerations.

At the federal level, corporations must navigate income tax filings (Form 1120 for C-corps, 1120-S for S-corps, 1065 for partnerships), estimated tax payments, and compliance with the Internal Revenue Code. State taxes add another layer of complexity, with varying corporate income tax rates, franchise taxes, allocation and apportionment rules, and nexus rules that determine taxability based on physical or economic presence. Local taxes, including property and municipal business taxes, further complicate the compliance matrix. International operations introduce transfer pricing regulations, withholding taxes, and compliance with the OECD's Base Erosion and Profit Shifting (BEPS) framework.

Sales tax is another critical area where controllers must be vigilant. The 2018 South Dakota v. Wayfair Supreme Court decision expanded sales tax obligations for remote sellers, requiring businesses to collect and remit taxes in states where they have economic nexus—even without a physical presence. Controllers must implement systems to track sales by jurisdiction, apply correct tax rates, and file returns accurately to avoid penalties.

> *Tax compliance isn't just about filing returns—it's about embedding tax awareness into every financial decision to avoid costly surprises.*

Key responsibilities for controllers in tax compliance include:

- Ensuring accurate and timely filing of all tax returns

- Maintaining documentation for audits and disputes

- Monitoring legislative changes impacting tax obligations

- Collaborating with external tax advisors for complex filings

- Implementing internal controls to prevent errors or fraud

FEDERAL AND STATE COMPLIANCE

Federal tax compliance begins with determining the correct entity classification (C-corp, S-corp, partnership, etc.), as this dictates filing requirements, deductions, and tax rates. C-corporations face double taxation risk (corporate tax + shareholder dividends), while pass-through entities like S-corps and LLCs flow income directly to owners' personal returns. Controllers must ensure accurate book-to-tax adjustments, such as reconciling GAAP financials with taxable income by accounting for differences in depreciation (MACRS vs. straight-line), amortization, and reserves.

State tax compliance is equally demanding. Many states impose franchise taxes based on revenue, capital, or a combination, while others levy corporate income taxes with varying apportionment rules. For example, California uses a single-sales factor apportionment, while Texas relies on gross receipts for franchise tax calculations. Controllers must track payroll, property, and sales data by state to allocate income correctly and avoid underpayment penalties.

Multistate operations require careful nexus analysis— physical presence (employees, offices) or economic nexus (exceeding sales thresholds) can trigger filing obligations. Voluntary disclosure agreements (VDAs) may be necessary if historical filings were missed, allowing companies to come into compliance while limiting back taxes and penalties. Sales tax nexus follows similar rules, with economic thresholds typically set at $100,000 in sales or 200 transactions annually.

Tax credits and incentives can offset liabilities but require proactive management. R\&D credits, energy efficiency incentives, and job creation credits vary by state and often involve complex documentation. Controllers should work with tax advisors to identify qualifying activities and maintain supporting records.

INTERNATIONAL TAX AND TRANSFER PRICING

Global operations introduce transfer pricing, withholding taxes, and foreign reporting requirements. Transfer pricing regulations (IRC §482) mandate that intercompany transactions (e.g., licensing, services, loans) be conducted at arm's length to prevent profit shifting. Controllers must maintain contemporaneous documentation, including benchmarking studies, to justify pricing methodologies (comparable uncontrolled price, cost-plus, etc.). Failure to comply can lead to double taxation or penalties under local tax authorities.

The Tax Cuts and Jobs Act (TCJA) introduced GILTI (Global Intangible Low-Taxed Income) and FDII (Foreign-Derived Intangible Income) regimes, taxing foreign earnings at reduced rates but adding reporting complexity. Controllers must track Subpart F income, CFC (Controlled Foreign Corporation) filings, and BEAT (Base Erosion Anti-Abuse Tax) exposures.

Withholding taxes apply to cross-border payments (dividends, interest, royalties), with rates often reduced by tax treaties. Companies must validate treaty eligibility via W-8BEN forms and monitor changes (e.g., OECD's Pillar Two global minimum tax). VAT/GST compliance is another critical area, requiring registration, invoicing, and return filings in jurisdictions where services or goods are supplied.

SALES AND PAYROLL TAX MANAGEMENT

Sales tax compliance hinges on accurate rate determination, exemption certificate management, and timely filings. Controllers should automate tax calculation software (e.g., Avalara, Vertex) to integrate with ERP systems, reducing manual errors. Audits are common, so maintaining detailed records of exempt sales (resale certificates, government entities) is essential.

Payroll taxes (federal/state income tax withholding, FICA, FUTA, SUTA) require precise calculation and remittance. Misclassification of employees vs. contractors (per IRS §530 safe harbor rules) can trigger audits and back taxes. Controllers must ensure proper withholding for equity compensation (RSUs, NQSOs) and fringe benefits correctly.

TAX STRATEGY AND CONTROVERSY

Proactive tax planning aligns compliance with business goals. Strategies include:

- Entity Structuring: Choosing between C-corp vs. pass-through based on investor exit plans.

- Tax Elections: Accelerating deductions via IRC §179 expensing or deferring income.

- Interest Expense Limitation (IRC §163(j): Planning to maximize the interest expense deduction on the company's debt. Many of us have had nasty surprises with this section of the tax code, due to the high levels of debt in portfolio company's.

- M&A Tax Planning: Structuring deals as asset vs. stock purchases to optimize step-ups.

- Dispute Resolution: Responding to IRS or state notices, negotiating settlements.

> *The best tax strategy isn't about evasion—it's about making informed, defensible decisions that align with business objectives.*

Controllers must balance risk and reward, ensuring strategies withstand scrutiny while minimizing liabilities. Regular communication with PE sponsors, CFOs, and external advisors is key to navigating this ever-evolving landscape.

CHAPTER 12:

FINANCIAL SYSTEMS AND TECHNOLOGY

● ◆ ●

FINANCIAL SYSTEMS IN CONTROLLERSHIP

Financial systems are the backbone of any organization's accounting and reporting infrastructure. For financial controllers, selecting, implementing, and maintaining these systems is a critical responsibility that directly impacts efficiency, accuracy, and scalability. In today's fast-paced business environment, where private equity owned companies demand real-time insights and robust reporting, the right financial technology stack can mean the difference between seamless operations and costly inefficiencies. This chapter explores the key considerations for financial systems, from selection to optimization, while addressing the unique needs of PE-backed firms, venture capital funded startups, and founder-owned businesses. We'll also examine how controllers can leverage technology to streamline processes, enhance compliance, and support strategic decision-making.

THE ROLE OF FINANCIAL SYSTEMS IN CONTROLLERSHIP

Financial systems serve as the central hub for all accounting activities, from transactional processing to high-level reporting. For controllers, these systems must not only handle day-to-day bookkeeping but also provide the flexibility to adapt to evolving business needs, such as GAAP compliance, multi-entity consolidations, and investor reporting. A well-designed financial system reduces manual work, minimizes errors, and ensures data integrity—critical factors when dealing with PE sponsors who require precise, auditable financials for valuation and exit planning.

One of the primary challenges controllers face is balancing cost with functionality. While enterprise resource planning (ERP) systems like NetSuite, Oracle, Intacct or SAP offer comprehensive solutions, they may be overkill for smaller portfolio companies. Conversely, lightweight accounting software like QuickBooks, Xero, or Freshbooks may lack the scalability needed for rapid growth or complex transactions. The key is to assess the organization's current and future needs, including multi-currency support, intercompany eliminations, and integration with other business systems (e.g., CRM, payroll, or treasury management).

Another critical consideration is data security and access controls. PE firms often require segmented financial data for individual portfolio companies while maintaining oversight at the fund level. Controllers must ensure that role-based permissions are configured to prevent unauthorized access while allowing stakeholders—such as auditors, tax advisors, and PE sponsors—to retrieve necessary information efficiently.

> *A financial system is only as good as the processes it supports. Without clear workflows and internal controls, even the most advanced software can become a liability.*

Finally, controllers must stay ahead of technological advancements, such as cloud-based solutions, artificial intelligence for anomaly detection, and robotic process automation for repetitive tasks. These innovations can dramatically improve efficiency but require careful implementation to avoid disruption.

EVALUATING AND SELECTING THE RIGHT FINANCIAL SYSTEM

Choosing the right financial system is a strategic decision that requires input from multiple stakeholders, including IT, operations, and executive leadership. For PE-owned companies, the selection process may also include the sponsor's operational team, who often have preferences based on prior portfolio company experiences. Controllers should begin by conducting a thorough needs assessment, identifying pain points in the current system, and defining must-have versus nice-to-have features.

Key evaluation criteria include:

- Scalability – Can the system handle increased transaction volumes, additional entities, or international expansion?

- Integration Capabilities – Does it seamlessly connect with other critical systems (e.g., banking, payroll, or expense management)?

- Reporting Flexibility – Can it generate GAAP-compliant financials, management dashboards, and investor-specific reports?

- User-Friendliness – Is the interface intuitive for accounting staff, or will extensive training be required?

- Vendor Support – Does the provider offer reliable customer service, regular updates, and compliance with regulatory changes?

For PE-backed firms, controllers should also consider the system's ability to support mergers and acquisitions. A robust financial system should facilitate due diligence, post-merger integrations, and carve-out financials for divestitures. Additionally, cloud-based systems are increasingly favored for their remote accessibility, which is essential for decentralized teams and PE firms monitoring multiple portfolio companies.

Once a shortlist of systems is identified, controllers should request demos, speak with existing customers, and conduct pilot tests where feasible. It's also wise to involve the internal audit team early in the process to assess control implications.

IMPLEMENTATION BEST PRACTICES

Implementing a new financial system is a complex, often disruptive process that requires meticulous planning. Controllers must develop a detailed project plan, assigning clear responsibilities and setting realistic timelines. For PE-owned companies, implementation timelines may be aggressive due to reporting deadlines or impending audits, making phased rollouts a practical approach.

Data migration is one of the most critical and risky aspects of implementation. Historical financial data must be accurately transferred, mapped to the new system's structure, and validated for consistency. Controllers should work closely with IT and external consultants to ensure data integrity, particularly for multi-entity consolidations and intercompany transactions.

Training is another make-or-break factor. Even the best system will underperform if end-users don't understand its features. Controllers should organize role-specific training sessions, create user manuals, and designate "super-users" within the accounting team to serve as internal resources.

> *A successful implementation isn't just about going live— it's about ensuring the system is adopted, optimized, and continuously improved.*

Post-implementation, controllers should establish a feedback loop to identify and address any issues promptly. Regular system audits and performance reviews will help maximize ROI and ensure the solution remains aligned with business needs.

LEVERAGING TECHNOLOGY FOR ADVANCED FINANCIAL MANAGEMENT

Beyond core accounting functions, modern financial systems offer tools that can transform controllership. For example, automated workflows for accounts payable and accounts receivable can reduce processing times and improve cash flow visibility. AI-powered analytics can detect anomalies in real-time, flagging potential fraud or errors before they escalate.

For PE sponsors, dashboards with key performance indicators and portfolio-level metrics are invaluable. Controllers should work with their PE partners to customize reports that align with the fund's investment thesis, such as EBITDA trends, working capital efficiency, or covenant compliance.

Treasury management modules can also enhance cash forecasting accuracy by integrating bank feeds, payment schedules, and liquidity projections. This is particularly useful for leveraged companies with tight cash flow requirements.

MAINTAINING AND UPGRADING FINANCIAL SYSTEMS

Financial systems are not "set it and forget it" tools. Controllers must oversee regular maintenance, including software updates, security patches, and compliance with new accounting standards (e.g., ASC 842 for leases). For PE-owned companies, system upgrades may coincide with new portfolio additions or exit preparations, requiring careful coordination.

Controllers should also stay informed about emerging technologies, such as blockchain for audit trails or predictive analytics for budgeting. While not every innovation will be immediately applicable, understanding the landscape ensures the organization remains competitive.

In summary, financial systems are a strategic asset for controllers, particularly in PE-backed environments where precision, scalability, and reporting transparency are paramount. By selecting the right system, implementing it effectively, and continuously optimizing its use, controllers can drive operational excellence and add measurable value to their organizations.

CHAPTER 13:

MERGERS AND ACQUISITIONS: THE BUY SIDE

● ◆ ●

THE CONTROLLER'S PIVOTAL ROLE IN ACQUISITIONS

Mergers and acquisitions are transformative events for any company, and the financial controller plays a critical role in ensuring their success. Unlike routine accounting functions, M&A transactions demand a unique blend of strategic thinking, financial acumen, and operational oversight. The controller must not only assess the financial health of a target company but also ensure seamless integration post-acquisition. This involves coordinating with private equity sponsors, legal teams, and operational leaders to align financial reporting, internal controls, and accounting policies. The buy-side process, particularly in private equity-owned companies, requires meticulous due diligence, accurate valuation, and structured financing. Controllers must also anticipate risks, from hidden liabilities to cultural mismatches, and develop mitigation strategies. Given the high stakes—where a single oversight can lead to financial losses or integration failures—the controller's expertise is indispensable.

One of the most challenging aspects of buy-side M&A is balancing speed with thoroughness. Private equity firms often operate under tight deadlines, pressuring controllers to expedite due diligence without compromising accuracy. This requires a structured approach, leveraging checklists, standardized workflows, and cross-functional collaboration. The controller must also ensure that all financial data adheres to GAAP, as deviations can lead to post-closing adjustments or even deal renegotiations. Additionally, the target's historical financials must be scrutinized for consistency, ensuring that revenue recognition, expense categorization, and reserve policies align with the acquirer's standards. Any discrepancies must be flagged early to avoid surprises during integration.

> *In M\&A, the financial controller is the gatekeeper of truth. Their ability to uncover risks and opportunities in a target's financials can make or break a deal.*

Beyond the numbers, the controller must evaluate the target's financial systems and processes. Outdated or incompatible systems can lead to costly post-merger integration challenges, requiring immediate upgrades or replacements. The controller should assess whether the target's accounting software, ERP systems, and reporting tools can integrate smoothly with the acquiring company's infrastructure. If not, a detailed transition plan must be developed, including data migration protocols and employee training. Another critical consideration is internal controls, as weaknesses in the target's control environment can expose the acquirer to fraud or compliance risks. The controller must document these gaps and recommend remediation steps before closing.

Finally, the controller plays a key role in structuring the deal. Whether it's an asset purchase, stock purchase, or merger, each structure has distinct tax, legal, and accounting implications. The controller must work closely with tax advisors to optimize the deal's structure, minimizing liabilities while ensuring compliance. They must also model various scenarios, assessing how different financing options (debt, equity, or seller financing) will impact the combined entity's balance sheet and cash flow. Post-closing, the controller oversees the purchase price allocation, ensuring that intangible assets, goodwill, and liabilities are accurately recorded under GAAP. This process directly affects future financial reporting and tax obligations, making it a high-priority task.

DUE DILIGENCE: UNCOVERING RISKS AND OPPORTUNITIES

Due diligence is the backbone of any successful acquisition, and the controller is at the forefront of this process. Unlike routine audits, due diligence requires a forward-looking perspective, identifying not just historical inaccuracies but also future risks. The controller must review the target's financial statements, tax returns, and internal reports, searching for red flags such as irregular revenue patterns, unrecorded liabilities, or aggressive accounting practices. Special attention should be paid to contingent liabilities such as pending litigation, environmental claims, or warranty obligations, which may not be correctly or fully reflected in the financials. These hidden risks can significantly impact the deal's valuation and post-closing financial health.

Another critical area of due diligence is working capital analysis. The controller must verify the target's net working capital to ensure it aligns with industry benchmarks and the acquirer's expectations. Significant deviations may indicate operational inefficiencies or accounting anomalies. For example, inflated accounts receivable could signal collection issues, while bloated inventory might suggest obsolescence risks. The controller should also assess the quality of the target's assets, confirming that fixed assets are properly maintained and intangible assets (like patents or trademarks) are legally protected. Any discrepancies between reported values and actual conditions must be addressed before closing.

> *Due diligence isn't just about finding problems—it's about understanding the target's true financial DNA.*

The controller and others in the company must also evaluate the target's revenue streams and customer contracts. Recurring revenue models, long-term contracts, and customer concentration risks all influence the target's valuation and sustainability. For instance, if a single customer accounts for 40% of revenue, the acquirer faces significant dependency risk. The controller should review contract terms, payment schedules, and renewal rates to assess stability. Additionally, they must confirm that revenue recognition policies comply with GAAP, particularly for subscription-based or milestone-driven businesses. Misapplied revenue recognition can lead to restatements post-acquisition, damaging credibility with investors and lenders.

Tax due diligence is another cornerstone of the process. The controller must scrutinize the target's tax filings, ensuring compliance with federal, state, and local regulations. Unpaid taxes, unresolved audits, or aggressive tax positions can trigger post-closing liabilities. Transfer pricing arrangements—especially in cross-border deals—must be reviewed for compliance with OECD guidelines. The controller should also assess the target's tax attributes, such as net operating losses or tax credits, which may be valuable to the acquirer. Any identified issues should be factored into the deal's terms, either through price adjustments or indemnification clauses.

Finally, the controller, in conjunction with their HR partners, must assess the target's human resources and payroll systems. Employee-related liabilities—such as unpaid bonuses, pension obligations, or pending labor disputes—can create unexpected financial burdens. The controller should review payroll records, benefit plans, and employment contracts to identify potential exposures. Additionally, they must evaluate whether the target's compensation structure aligns with the acquirer's policies, as misalignment can lead to integration challenges. Cultural fit is another intangible yet critical factor; the finance teams of both companies must be able to collaborate effectively post-merger.

STRUCTURING THE DEAL: FINANCIAL AND TAX CONSIDERATIONS

Once due diligence is complete, the controller must collaborate with legal and tax advisors to structure the deal optimally. The choice between an asset purchase and a stock purchase has profound implications for both parties. In an asset purchase, the acquirer can selectively acquire assets while avoiding unwanted liabilities, often resulting in a step-up in tax basis for depreciation purposes. However, this structure may trigger higher transaction taxes and require third-party consents for asset transfers. In contrast, a stock purchase simplifies the process by transferring ownership of the entire entity, but the acquirer inherits all liabilities—known and unknown. The controller must weigh these trade-offs carefully, aligning the structure with the acquirer's strategic and financial goals.

Financing the acquisition is another critical consideration. Private equity-owned companies often use a combination of debt and equity, and the controller must model the impact on the combined entity's leverage ratios and cash flow. If debt financing is used, the controller must ensure that the target's cash flow can service the additional debt without straining operations. They should also review existing debt covenants to avoid triggering acceleration clauses. Seller financing—where the seller provides a loan to the buyer—can be advantageous but requires careful negotiation of terms. The controller must also assess the tax implications of financing structures, as interest deductibility varies by jurisdiction.

> *The right deal structure can unlock value; the wrong one can bury the acquirer in unforeseen liabilities.*

Purchase price adjustments are another area where the controller's expertise is vital. Most deals include mechanisms to adjust the final price based on closing-date working capital or other financial metrics. The controller must establish clear definitions and measurement methodologies in the purchase agreement to avoid disputes. They should also model various scenarios to anticipate potential adjustments, ensuring the acquirer isn't overpaying. Earn-outs—where additional payments are tied to future performance—are common in private equity deals but require precise structuring to align incentives. The controller must ensure that earn-out targets are measurable, achievable, and properly documented.

Tax structuring is equally crucial. The controller must work with tax advisors to optimize the deal's tax efficiency, considering aspects like step-up elections, NOL utilization, and jurisdiction-specific incentives. In cross-border transactions, withholding taxes, treaty benefits, and permanent establishment risks must be evaluated. The controller should also plan for post-closing tax integration, ensuring that the combined entity complies with all filing requirements. Failure to address these issues can result in double taxation, penalties, or missed opportunities for tax savings.

Finally, the controller must prepare for the accounting implications of the deal. Under GAAP, the acquirer must perform a purchase price allocation, assigning the purchase price to tangible and intangible assets under ASC 805, with any residual amount recorded as goodwill. The controller must engage valuation specialists to appraise assets like customer relationships, technology, and brand value. This allocation affects future depreciation, amortization, and impairment testing, directly impacting financial statements. The controller must also assess whether the acquisition triggers any changes to accounting policies, such as revenue recognition or lease accounting, requiring updates to internal controls and systems.

POST-ACQUISITION INTEGRATION: ENSURING A SMOOTH TRANSITION

The real work begins after the deal closes, and the controller is central to ensuring a successful integration. Financial integration process must be meticulously planned to avoid disruptions to operations and reporting. The first step is aligning the target's chart of accounts with the acquirer's, enabling consolidated financial reporting. The controller must also harmonize accounting policies, ensuring consistent application of GAAP across both entities. Any differences in revenue recognition, expense categorization, or reserve methodologies must be reconciled to prevent misstatements. This often requires retraining the target's finance team and updating their systems to match the acquirer's standards.

Systems integration is another critical task. If the target uses different ERP or accounting software, the controller must decide whether to migrate them to the acquirer's system or maintain parallel systems temporarily. Data migration is a complex process, requiring validation to ensure accuracy. The controller should establish a timeline for integration, prioritizing critical functions like accounts payable, payroll, and financial reporting. They must also implement robust controls over the transition period to prevent errors or fraud. Any delays or missteps in systems integration can lead to reporting lags, audit findings, or operational inefficiencies.

> *Integration isn't just a technical alignment—it's about merging two cultures into one cohesive finance function.*

People integration is often overlooked but equally important. The controller must assess the target's finance team, identifying key personnel to retain and skill gaps to address. Cultural alignment is essential; conflicting work styles or resistance to change can derail integration. The controller should facilitate cross-team collaboration, organizing joint meetings and training sessions to foster unity. Clear communication is vital—employees from both companies need to understand the integration roadmap, their roles, and how performance will be measured. Retaining top talent often requires retention bonuses or career development assurances, which the controller must budget for.

Internal controls must be strengthened post-acquisition. The target's control environment may have been adequate as a standalone entity but could fall short under the acquirer's standards. The controller should conduct a controls assessment, identifying gaps and implementing remediation plans. This includes segregating duties, enhancing approval workflows, and upgrading fraud detection measures. The controller must also ensure that the combined entity complies with SOX requirements if applicable. Strong controls not only mitigate risks but also build confidence among private equity sponsors and lenders.

Finally, the controller must monitor the acquisition's financial performance against expectations. This involves tracking synergies—both cost savings and revenue enhancements— to validate the deal's rationale. The controller should develop post-acquisition KPIs, comparing actual results to pre-deal projections. Any variances must be analyzed and addressed promptly. Regular updates should be provided to private equity sponsors, highlighting progress and challenges. The controller's ability to deliver transparent, accurate post-merger reporting is critical to maintaining stakeholder trust and securing future investment.

COMMON PITFALLS AND BEST PRACTICES

Even the most experienced controllers can encounter pitfalls in buy-side M&A. One common mistake is underestimating the complexity of integration. Some acquirers focus solely on the deal's financials, neglecting operational and cultural integration until it's too late. The controller must advocate for a holistic approach, ensuring that integration planning begins during due diligence. Another frequent error is over-reliance on the target's historical financials without considering forward-looking risks. Market shifts, regulatory changes, or technological disruptions can quickly render past performance irrelevant. The controller should incorporate scenario analysis into due diligence, stress-testing the target's business model under various conditions.

> *The best controllers don't just report history—they anticipate the future.*

Communication breakdowns are another recurring issue. M&A deals involve multiple stakeholders—private equity firms, lenders, legal teams, and operational leaders—each with competing priorities. The controller must act as a bridge, ensuring that financial insights are communicated clearly and consistently. Regular status updates, dashboards, and risk registers can help keep everyone aligned. Additionally, the controller should document all assumptions, decisions, and action items to create accountability. Ambiguity in roles or expectations can lead to delays and finger-pointing post-closing.

Best practices can mitigate these risks. First, the controller should develop a standardized M&A playbook, outlining due diligence checklists, integration templates, and risk assessment frameworks. This ensures consistency across deals and accelerates the process. Second, they should foster strong relationships with external advisors—legal, tax, and valuation experts—who can provide specialized insights. Third, the controller must prioritize change management, recognizing that successful integration depends on people as much as processes. Finally, they should conduct post-mortem reviews after each deal, identifying lessons learned and refining strategies for future transactions.

By mastering these principles, controllers can transform M&A from a high-risk gamble into a value-creating engine. Their ability to navigate financial complexities, mitigate risks, and drive seamless integration makes them indispensable in the buy-side process. For private equity-owned companies, where deals are frequent and stakes are high, a skilled controller is the ultimate safeguard against costly missteps.

CHAPTER 14:

MERGERS AND ACQUISITIONS: THE SELL SIDE

• ♦ •

INTRODUCTION TO SELL-SIDE M&A

Sell-side mergers and acquisitions represent one of the most complex yet rewarding responsibilities of a financial controller. Unlike buy-side transactions, where the focus is on acquiring new businesses, sell-side M&A involves preparing a company for divestiture, spinoff, or outright sale. The financial controller plays a pivotal role in ensuring that the company's financials are audit-ready, compliant with GAAP, and presented in a manner that maximizes valuation. Private equity-owned companies, in particular, require meticulous preparation due to the high expectations of sponsors seeking optimal returns on their investments. The process begins with understanding the strategic rationale behind the sale—whether it's a portfolio optimization, an exit strategy, or a response to market conditions. From there, the financial team must align financial reporting, internal controls, and due diligence processes to meet buyer expectations.

One of the first steps in sell-side M&A is assembling a cross-functional team, including legal, tax, and operational leaders, to ensure all aspects of the transaction are addressed. The financial controller must oversee the preparation of historical financial statements, ensuring they are free from material misstatements and adhere to GAAP. This includes reconciling any discrepancies in accounts payable, accounts receivable, and payroll records. Additionally, the controller must ensure that all financial systems are up to date and capable of producing the granular data required for due diligence. Private equity sponsors often demand detailed cash flow forecasts and pro forma financials to demonstrate the company's growth potential. The financial controller must also anticipate buyer concerns, such as contingent liabilities, tax exposures, or pending litigation, and address them proactively.

> *A well-prepared sell-side financial package is the difference between a smooth transaction and a deal that collapses under scrutiny.*

Another critical aspect of sell-side M&A is understanding the different types of buyers and their expectations. Strategic buyers, such as competitors or industry consolidators, often focus on synergies and integration potential. Financial buyers, including private equity firms, prioritize cash flow, leverage capacity, and exit multiples. The financial controller must tailor financial presentations to highlight the metrics most relevant to each buyer type. For example, EBITDA adjustments, working capital trends, and capital expenditure requirements may be scrutinized differently depending on the buyer's investment thesis. The controller must also ensure that all financial reporting consolidations—

especially in cases where subsidiaries or international entities are involved—are accurate and defensible. Transfer pricing policies, intercompany eliminations, and tax implications must be thoroughly documented to avoid post-closing disputes.

Finally, the financial controller must manage the tension between speed and accuracy. Private equity sponsors often push for accelerated timelines to capitalize on favorable market conditions, but rushing the process can lead to overlooked liabilities or valuation discounts. A disciplined approach to financial readiness—including pre-sale audits, quality of earnings reports, and mock due diligence—can mitigate these risks. The controller must also prepare for post-closing adjustments, such as working capital true-ups or earn-out calculations, which can significantly impact the final sale price. By mastering these elements, the financial controller ensures that the company is positioned for a successful and lucrative exit.

PREPARING FINANCIAL STATEMENTS FOR SALE

The foundation of any sell-side M&A transaction is the preparation of accurate, GAAP-compliant financial statements. Buyers and their advisors will scrutinize every line item, so the financial controller must ensure that the books are immaculate. This begins with a thorough review of the general ledger, ensuring that all journal entries are properly supported and that all reconciling items in accounts payable, accounts receivable, and payroll have been resolved. Historical financials should be restated, if necessary, to correct any prior-period errors, and all material transactions should be clearly documented. Private equity sponsors often require carve-out financials if only a division or subsidiary is being sold, which adds another layer of complexity. The financial controller must work closely with auditors to ensure that these statements are audit-ready, as buyers will likely commission their own quality of earnings review.

One of the most challenging aspects of preparing financial statements for sale is addressing non-recurring or unusual items. Buyers will adjust EBITDA to reflect the company's normalized earnings, so the financial controller must provide detailed explanations for one-time expenses, owner-related costs, or discretionary spending. For example, private equity-owned companies often have management fees, transaction expenses, or shareholder distributions that need to be adjusted out of EBITDA. The controller must also ensure that revenue recognition policies are consistently applied and well-documented, especially in industries with complex billing structures, such as SaaS or long-term contracts. Any deviations from GAAP must be disclosed, and the controller should be prepared to defend the company's accounting policies during due diligence.

Another critical consideration is the treatment of working capital in the sale agreement. Buyers typically expect the target company to deliver a "normalized" level of working capital at closing, and deviations can result in purchase price adjustments. The financial controller must establish a working capital target—often based on a 12-month average—and ensure that the company's balance sheet aligns with this benchmark at closing. This requires close coordination with the accounts payable and accounts receivable teams to manage payment timing, inventory levels, and collections. The controller should also anticipate seasonal fluctuations and ensure that the working capital calculation methodology is clearly defined in the purchase agreement to avoid post-closing disputes.

Tax considerations are equally important when preparing financial statements for sale. The financial controller must ensure that all federal, state, and local tax filings are up to date and that any potential exposures are quantified. In cross-border transactions, transfer pricing documentation must be robust to withstand scrutiny from tax authorities in multiple jurisdictions. The controller should also assess the tax implications of the sale structure (asset sale, stock sale, or merger) as this can significantly impact both the buyer and seller. For example, asset sales may trigger higher tax liabilities for the seller but provide step-up benefits for the buyer. The financial controller must work closely with tax advisors to model these scenarios and optimize the tax efficiency of the transaction.

Finally, the financial controller must prepare for the intense scrutiny that comes with due diligence. Buyers will request access to detailed financial records, contracts, and operational data, often through a virtual data room. The controller must ensure that all documents are organized, indexed, and redacted as necessary to protect sensitive information. Common areas of focus include customer contracts (for revenue recognition), lease agreements (for ASC 842 compliance), and employee benefit plans (for liability assessments). The controller should also be prepared to respond to due diligence inquiries promptly and accurately, as delays can erode buyer confidence. By meticulously preparing financial statements and supporting documentation, the financial controller minimizes deal risk and enhances the company's valuation.

MANAGING DUE DILIGENCE AND BUYER INQUIRIES

Due diligence is the make-or-break phase of any sell-side M&A transaction, and the financial controller is at the center of this process. Buyers and their advisors will pore over financial records, contracts, and operational data to validate the company's performance and uncover potential risks. The financial controller must anticipate these inquiries and ensure that all requested information is accurate, consistent, and readily available. This begins with setting up a secure virtual data room, where documents are organized into logical categories—financial statements, tax filings, customer contracts, employment agreements, and more. The controller should also establish a clear protocol for responding to due diligence requests, designating point persons for different functional areas to avoid bottlenecks.

One of the most critical components of due diligence is the quality of earnings review, which buyers use to assess the sustainability and reliability of the company's earnings. The financial controller must ensure that EBITDA adjustments are well-documented and defensible, as buyers will challenge any add-backs that appear aggressive or unsupported. Common adjustments include non-recurring expenses, owner-related costs, and discretionary spending, but the controller must be prepared to justify each item with underlying documentation. For example, if the company has historically paid above-market salaries to family members, the buyer may argue that these costs should not be adjusted out of EBITDA. The controller must work closely with the CFO and private equity sponsors to establish a reasonable adjustment framework that aligns with market standards.

Another area of intense scrutiny is the company's internal controls and compliance with GAAP. Buyers will assess whether the financial reporting processes are robust enough to prevent material misstatements, especially in private equity-owned companies where there may have been aggressive cost-cutting. The financial controller should be prepared to provide documentation of control frameworks, such as segregation of duties, approval hierarchies, and month-end close procedures. Any material weaknesses or significant deficiencies identified in prior audits must be disclosed and explained, along with remediation plan. Buyers will also examine the company's accounting policies, particularly in areas such as revenue recognition, inventory valuation, and lease accounting, to ensure they comply with GAAP and industry norms.

Legal and contractual due diligence is another critical area where the financial controller plays a supporting role. Buyers will review all material contracts—customer agreements, supplier contracts, leases, and debt instruments—to assess potential liabilities or restrictions. The controller must ensure that all contracts are up to date, properly executed, and free from onerous terms that could impact the transaction. For example, change-of-control provisions in customer contracts could trigger termination rights, while outstanding litigation or regulatory investigations could create contingent liabilities. The financial controller should work closely with legal counsel to identify and quantify these risks, as they can significantly impact the deal's terms or valuation.

Finally, the financial controller must manage the human element of due diligence. Buyer teams often include accountants, lawyers, and operational experts who will interview key personnel, including the controller themselves. These interviews can be high-pressure, as buyers probe for inconsistencies or undisclosed risks. The controller must strike a balance between transparency and discretion, providing accurate information without volunteering unnecessary details that could derail the deal. It's also essential to maintain morale among the finance team, as prolonged due diligence can be stressful. By leading with professionalism and preparedness, the financial controller ensures that the due diligence process proceeds smoothly, building buyer confidence and preserving deal momentum.

NEGOTIATING DEAL TERMS AND POST-CLOSING ADJUSTMENTS

Once due diligence is complete, the financial controller shifts focus to assisting the PE sponsor and management in negotiating deal terms and preparing for post-closing adjustments. The purchase agreement will outline key financial considerations, including the purchase price, working capital targets, indemnification provisions, and earn-out structures. The financial controller must ensure that these terms are clearly defined and that the company's interests are protected. For example, the working capital adjustment mechanism should specify which balance sheet accounts are included, the calculation methodology, and the timeline for post-closing true-ups. Ambiguities in these provisions can lead to costly disputes, so the controller must work closely with legal counsel to draft precise language.

One of the most contentious areas of negotiation is the definition of "normalized" working capital. Buyers often argue for lower targets to reduce the effective purchase price, while sellers seek higher targets to maximize proceeds. The financial controller must provide historical data to support the company's working capital needs, demonstrating seasonality trends and operational requirements. For example, a manufacturing company may require higher inventory levels ahead of peak sales periods, and this should be reflected in the target. The controller should also ensure that the purchase agreement includes a dispute resolution mechanism, such as a neutral accounting firm, to adjudicate any disagreements over working capital adjustments.

Earn-outs are another common feature of sell-side M&A, particularly when there is disagreement over the company's future performance. These provisions tie a portion of the purchase price to the achievement of post-closing milestones, such as revenue targets or EBITDA thresholds. The financial controller must ensure that earn-out metrics are clearly defined, measurable, and within the seller's control. For example, if the earn-out is based on revenue growth, the agreement should specify whether it includes organic growth only or allows for acquisitions. The controller should also advocate for protections against buyer actions that could undermine earn-out achievement, such as diverting resources or changing business strategies. Detailed financial models and scenario analyses can help both parties agree on realistic earn-out structures.

Tax considerations are also critical during deal negotiations. The financial controller must understand the tax structure of the transaction—whether it's an asset sale, stock sale, or merger—and its implications for both parties. In an asset sale, for example, the seller may face higher tax liabilities due to recapture of depreciation, while the buyer benefits from a step-up in asset basis. The controller should work with tax advisors to model these scenarios and negotiate allocations of purchase price among assets to optimize tax outcomes. Additionally, the controller must ensure that all pre-closing tax liabilities, such as unpaid payroll taxes or sales taxes, are properly accounted for and that indemnification provisions cover any post-closing tax assessments.

Post-closing, the financial controller's role shifts to executing the transition smoothly. This includes finalizing the working capital true-up, calculating earn-out payments, and ensuring compliance with any ongoing reporting obligations. The controller must also oversee the integration of financial systems, if applicable, and assist with the transfer of accounting records to the buyer. In private equity-backed deals, the controller may be involved in distributing sale proceeds to investors and reconciling final fund-level financials. Throughout this phase, clear communication and meticulous record-keeping are essential to avoid disputes and ensure a positive outcome for all parties. By mastering these aspects of deal negotiations and post-closing adjustments, the financial controller plays a pivotal role in maximizing value and minimizing risk in sell-side M&A.

LESSONS FROM SELL-SIDE TRANSACTIONS

The best way to understand the complexities of sell-side M&A is to examine examples where financial controllers significant challenges. One involved a mid-sized manufacturing company owned by a private equity firm. The controller discovered mid-due diligence that a key customer contract, representing 30% of revenue, had an auto-renewal clause that the buyer argued was unfavorable. The controller worked with legal counsel to renegotiate the contract terms before closing, preserving the deal's valuation. This highlights the importance of proactive contract review and the controller's role in mitigating risks that could derail a transaction.

Another example involves a software company undergoing a carve-out sale from a larger parent entity. The financial controller had to prepare standalone financial statements for the division, which required allocating shared costs, such as corporate overhead and R\&D expenses, in a manner that was both defensible and attractive to buyers. The controller developed a detailed cost-allocation methodology, supported by historical data, and worked with auditors to validate the approach. This case underscores the importance of meticulous financial reporting in carve-out transactions, where buyers demand transparency and accuracy in assessing a division's true profitability.

A third example comes from a retail chain being sold to a strategic buyer. During due diligence, the buyer identified discrepancies in inventory valuation, which led to a downward adjustment in the purchase price. The financial controller realized too late that the company's inventory tracking system had not been properly reconciled to the general ledger. This costly oversight could have been avoided with stronger internal controls and pre-sale audit procedures. The lesson here is clear: financial controllers must ensure that all balance sheet accounts, especially inventory and receivables, are fully reconciled and audit-ready before entering into a sale process.

In another case, a healthcare services company faced a post-closing dispute over working capital adjustments. The buyer argued that accounts payable had been understated at closing, while the seller contended that the buyer had delayed payments to manipulate the adjustment. The financial controller had failed to document the timing of invoice approvals before closing, making it difficult to resolve the disagreement. This scenario emphasizes the need for controllers to maintain detailed records of pre-closing transactions and to establish clear, mutually agreed-upon definitions for working capital calculations.

Finally, a successful example involves a financial controller who assisted in the sale of a logistics company to a private equity buyer. Recognizing that the buyer was highly focused on cash flow, the controller prepared detailed cash conversion cycle analyses and demonstrated how operational improvements could unlock additional working capital efficiency. This proactive approach not only justified a higher valuation but also positioned the controller for a leadership role in the post-acquisition integration. The takeaway is that financial controllers who understand their buyers' priorities and tailor their financial presentations accordingly can significantly enhance deal outcomes.

These examples illustrate the multifaceted role of the financial controller in sell-side M&A. From contract renegotiations to carve-out financials, from inventory reconciliations to working capital disputes, the controller's expertise and attention to detail are critical to navigating these complexities. By learning from these examples, controllers can anticipate challenges, implement best practices, and drive successful transactions that maximize value for all stakeholders.

CHAPTER 15:

ANNUAL FINANCIAL AUDITS

● ◆ ●

THE ANNUAL FINANCIAL AUDIT

The annual financial audit is one of the most critical processes a financial controller oversees. It serves as an independent verification of a company's financial health, ensuring accuracy, compliance, and transparency for stakeholders—including private equity sponsors, lenders, and regulatory bodies. A well-executed audit not only validates financial statements but also strengthens investor confidence, mitigates risk, and identifies areas for operational improvement. However, the process can be daunting, especially for controllers in private equity-backed companies where scrutiny is high, timelines are tight, and expectations are stringent. This chapter provides a comprehensive guide to navigating the annual audit, from preparation to execution and post-audit follow-up. We will explore best practices, common pitfalls, and strategies to streamline the process while maintaining compliance with GAAP and other regulatory requirements.

UNDERSTANDING THE PURPOSE AND IMPORTANCE OF THE ANNUAL AUDIT

The annual audit is not merely a compliance exercise—it is a vital tool for ensuring financial integrity of the organization. External auditors provide an independent assessment of whether financial statements present a true and fair view of the company's financial position, performance, and cash flows in accordance with GAAP. For private equity-owned companies, audits are particularly crucial because they often serve as a key due diligence checkpoint before exits, refinancing, or additional capital raises. Lenders also rely on audited financials to assess creditworthiness, making the audit a cornerstone of financial credibility.

Beyond compliance, audits help uncover inefficiencies, control weaknesses, or even fraud. A well-conducted audit can reveal discrepancies in revenue recognition, improper expense categorization, or lapses in internal controls— issues that, if left unaddressed, could lead to financial misstatements or regulatory penalties. Additionally, private equity sponsors use audit findings to evaluate management performance, making it imperative for controllers to ensure a smooth and error-free process. The audit also serves as a learning opportunity, providing insights into accounting policies, process improvements, and best practices that can enhance future financial reporting.

One of the biggest challenges controllers face is managing the expectations of multiple stakeholders. Private equity firms often demand granular detail and rapid turnaround times, while auditors require thorough documentation and adherence to strict timelines. Balancing these demands requires meticulous planning, clear communication, and a proactive approach to resolving issues before they escalate. Controllers must also be prepared to defend accounting judgments, particularly in areas involving estimates such as revenue recognition, lease accounting, acquisition valuations and the related purchase price accounting or fair value measurements. A strong understanding of GAAP and the ability to articulate the rationale behind accounting policies is essential in these discussions.

> *An audit is not just about checking boxes—it's about telling the financial story of the company with accuracy and transparency.*

To maximize the value of the audit, controllers should view it as a collaborative process rather than an adversarial one. Building a strong relationship with auditors, providing them with clear and organized documentation, and addressing their queries promptly can significantly reduce friction and delays. Proactive engagement with auditors during the year—such as through interim testing or pre-audit meetings—can also help identify potential issues early, allowing for smoother year-end close. Ultimately, the goal is to emerge from the audit with clean financials, strengthened controls, and actionable insights that drive business improvement.

PREPARING FOR THE AUDIT: KEY STEPS AND BEST PRACTICES

Preparation is the cornerstone of a successful audit. The more organized and proactive the controller is, the smoother the process will be. Ideally, audit preparation should begin months in advance, particularly for private equity-backed companies where audits are often tied to tight reporting deadlines for investor updates or debt covenant compliance. The first step is to establish a detailed audit timeline, outlining key milestones such as preliminary audit planning, interim testing, year-end close, and final audit fieldwork. This timeline should be shared with all relevant departments, including finance, accounting, legal, and operations, to ensure alignment and accountability.

One of the most critical preparatory tasks is ensuring that all supporting documentation is complete, accurate, and easily accessible. This includes:

- General ledger reconciliations

- Invoices

- Contracts

- Board minutes

- Any other records that substantiate financial transactions

Controllers should conduct a thorough pre-audit review to identify and resolve discrepancies before the auditors arrive. Special attention should be paid to high-risk areas such as revenue recognition, inventory valuation, and complex financial instruments, as these are often focal points for auditors. Implementing a standardized documentation checklist can help ensure nothing is overlooked.

Another key aspect of preparation is evaluating and strengthening internal controls. Auditors will assess the effectiveness of controls over financial reporting, so controllers should conduct a pre-audit control review to identify and remediate any weaknesses. This may involve:

- Updating segregation of duties

- Enhancing approval workflows

- Implementing new reconciliation procedures

For private equity portfolio companies, sponsors may have specific control frameworks that must be adhered to, so it's important to align with their expectations early in the process. Additionally, controllers should ensure that all accounting policies are well-documented and consistently applied, as auditors will scrutinize these for GAAP compliance.

Communication is another critical component of audit preparation. Controllers should:

- Schedule a kickoff meeting with the audit team to discuss scope, timelines, and expectations

- Provide regular status updates to senior management and private equity sponsors

- Clearly communicate significant changes (e.g., mergers, acquisitions, system implementations)

Finally, controllers should leverage technology to streamline the audit process. Cloud-based accounting systems, electronic document management, and data analytics tools can significantly reduce the burden of manual data gathering and improve accuracy. Many audit firms now use data extraction tools to analyze large datasets, so ensuring that financial systems can export data in compatible formats can save time and reduce back-and-forth. By investing in robust preparation, controllers can minimize disruptions to day-to-day operations, reduce audit fees, and achieve a more efficient and effective audit outcome.

MANAGING THE AUDIT PROCESS: EXECUTION TO COMPLETION

Once the audit begins, the controller's role shifts to active management of the process. This involves:

- Coordinating with auditors

- Addressing queries

- Ensuring prompt provision of requested information

The first phase typically involves a preliminary risk assessment, where auditors identify key areas of focus based on materiality, complexity, and past audit findings. Controllers should be prepared to walk auditors through the company's:

- Business model

- High level review of the audit and subsequent periods

- Significant transactions

- Changes in accounting policies

Fieldwork is the most intensive phase of the audit, where auditors:

- Test transactions

- Verify balances

- Evaluate internal controls

Controllers should:

- Assign a dedicated audit liaison (usually the assistant controller or accounting senior staff person)

- Establish daily/weekly check-ins with the audit team

- Maintain an issues log

One of the biggest challenges during fieldwork is managing the volume of requests while maintaining normal business operations. To mitigate this, controllers should:

- Establish a centralized repository for audit deliverables

- Set clear deadlines for internal teams

- Communicate early about unavailable information

As auditors complete their testing, they will typically identify adjustments or propose journal entries to correct misstatements. Controllers should:

- Review these carefully

- Assess materiality

- Be prepared to push back with justification if needed

The final phase involves preparing, reviewing and finalizing the financial statements and audit report. Controllers should:

- Conduct detailed proofreading

- Communicate last-minute adjustments to stakeholders

- Schedule a debrief with the audit team

COMMON AUDIT CHALLENGES AND HOW TO OVERCOME THEM

Despite thorough preparation, audits often present unexpected hurdles. Common challenges include:

GAAP Interpretation Differences

- Stay abreast of evolving accounting standards and discuss with the auditors technical team members

- Seek external guidance if necessary

- Engage third-party accounting advisory firms for complex topics

Incomplete Documentation

- Enforce a culture of documentation

- Implement a document management system

- Conduct regular internal audits – whether through an internal audit team, an outsourced team or using controller team members

Tight Deadlines

- Build buffer time into schedules

- Prioritize high-risk areas early

- Cross-train accounting staff

Internal Resistance

- Emphasize audit value in communications

- Offer training sessions

- Recognize team contributions

Cost Overruns

- Negotiate fees upfront

- Monitor progress against budget

- Consider phased approaches for major changes

POST-AUDIT FOLLOW-UP AND CONTINUOUS IMPROVEMENT

The audit doesn't end with the issuance of the financial statements. Post-audit activities include:

Addressing Findings

- Prioritize material weaknesses

- Create action plans with timelines
- Maintain transparent remediation trackers

Updating Policies

- Review audit adjustments
- Update accounting policies as needed
- Conduct targeted training

Process Evaluation

- Identify efficiency gains
- Solicit team (controllers team and the audit team) feedback
- Create standardized audit playbooks

Strategic Insights

- Share findings with department heads
- Drive cross-functional improvements
- Strengthen sponsor relationships

The best audits are those that don't just validate the past but also pave the way for a stronger financial future.

In summary, the annual audit is a multifaceted process that demands meticulous preparation, proactive management, and a commitment to continuous improvement. By understanding its purpose, preparing thoroughly, navigating execution challenges, and leveraging post-audit insights, controllers can transform what is often seen as a compliance burden into a strategic opportunity. For private equity-backed companies, where financial transparency is paramount, mastering the audit process is not just a responsibility—it's a competitive advantage.

CHAPTER 16:

TRANSFER PRICING AND INTERNATIONAL CONSIDERATIONS

● ◆ ●

UNDERSTANDING TRANSFER PRICING IN A GLOBAL CONTEXT

Transfer pricing is one of the most complex yet critical aspects of financial controllership for multinational companies, particularly those under private equity ownership. At its core, transfer pricing refers to the pricing of goods, services, and intangible assets exchanged between related entities within the same corporate group. The primary challenge lies in ensuring that these transactions are conducted at arm's length—meaning the prices should be consistent with what unrelated parties would agree upon in a free market. Failure to comply with transfer pricing regulations can lead to severe financial repercussions, including double taxation, penalties, and reputational damage. Private equity-owned companies must be especially vigilant, as their financial structures often involve intercompany transactions designed to optimize tax efficiency while maintaining compliance with international tax laws.

The arm's length principle is enshrined in the guidelines set by the Organization for Economic Co-operation and Development (OECD), which most countries follow. However, local tax authorities may have additional requirements, making compliance a moving target. For example, the U.S. Internal Revenue Service enforces strict documentation rules under Section 482 of the Internal Revenue Code, while the European Union has its own directives to prevent profit shifting. A financial controller must ensure that all intercompany transactions are properly documented, including detailed transfer pricing studies that justify the pricing methodology used. These studies typically involve benchmarking analyses, functional and risk assessments, and economic analyses to validate that the pricing aligns with market standards.

One of the most common transfer pricing methods is the Comparable Uncontrolled Price (CUP) method, which compares the price charged in a controlled transaction to that in an uncontrolled transaction between independent parties. Other methods include the Resale Price Method, Cost Plus Method, Transactional Net Margin Method (TNMM), and Profit Split Method. The choice of method depends on the nature of the transaction, availability of comparable data, and regulatory expectations. For instance, asset-light service companies may rely on TNMM, while manufacturing firms with significant tangible asset transfers might use the Cost Plus Method.

Private equity sponsors often push for tax-efficient structures, but controllers must balance these objectives with compliance risks. A poorly structured transfer pricing policy can trigger audits, leading to costly disputes with tax authorities. In extreme cases, companies may face transfer pricing adjustments that result in additional tax liabilities and interest charges. To mitigate these risks, controllers should work closely with tax advisors to develop a robust pricing strategy that aligns with both business objectives and regulatory requirements.

Transfer pricing isn't just a tax issue—it's a business strategy issue. Getting it wrong can erode profitability, but getting it right can create a competitive advantage.

- Conduct a thorough functional and risk analysis of intercompany transactions

- Select the most appropriate transfer pricing method based on transaction type

- Prepare and maintain comprehensive transfer pricing documentation

- Monitor changes in international tax laws and adjust policies accordingly

- Engage external tax advisors for complex cross-border transactions

COMPLIANCE WITH OECD AND LOCAL TAX REGULATIONS

Navigating the labyrinth of international tax regulations requires a deep understanding of both global standards and local nuances. The OECD Transfer Pricing Guidelines serve as the foundation, but many countries have their own interpretations and additional requirements. For example, countries like Brazil and India have stringent local filing requirements, including mandatory annual disclosure forms and advance pricing agreements (APAs). A financial controller must ensure that the company's transfer pricing policies are not only compliant with OECD principles but also tailored to the specific jurisdictions in which the company operates.

One of the biggest compliance hurdles is the Base Erosion and Profit Shifting (BEPS) initiative by the OECD, which aims to prevent multinational enterprises from artificially shifting profits to low-tax jurisdictions. BEPS Action 13 introduced the three-tiered documentation approach, consisting of a Master File, Local File, and Country-by-Country Reporting (CbCR). The Master File provides a high-level overview of the group's global business operations and transfer pricing policies, while the Local File contains detailed transactional data for each jurisdiction. CbCR, on the other hand, discloses revenue, profit, tax paid, and other key metrics for each country, enabling tax authorities to assess potential risks.

For private equity-owned companies, maintaining compliance with BEPS requirements is non-negotiable. Failure to file the necessary documentation can result in penalties and increased scrutiny from tax authorities. Controllers must ensure that all entities within the portfolio company's structure are aligned in their reporting and that data is consistently accurate across jurisdictions. This often requires collaboration with legal, tax, and operational teams to gather the required information. Additionally, some jurisdictions require the submission of transfer pricing documentation within strict deadlines, making timely preparation essential.

Another critical consideration is the potential for double taxation. If two countries dispute the arm's length nature of a transaction, they may impose conflicting adjustments, leading to the same income being taxed twice. To mitigate this risk, companies can pursue Mutual Agreement Procedures or APAs. An APA is a proactive agreement between a taxpayer and one or more tax authorities, establishing an acceptable transfer pricing methodology for future transactions. While APAs require significant effort to negotiate, they provide certainty and reduce audit risks.

- Align transfer pricing policies with OECD BEPS Action 13 requirements

- Prepare and submit Master File, Local File, and CbCR reports as needed

- Monitor local filing deadlines and documentation rules in all operating jurisdictions

- Evaluate the need for APAs to prevent double taxation disputes

- Coordinate with tax and legal teams to ensure consistent cross-border compliance

TREASURY AND CASH FLOW IMPLICATIONS OF TRANSFER PRICING

Transfer pricing doesn't just affect tax liabilities—it also has significant implications for treasury management and cash flow. Intercompany transactions influence liquidity, working capital, and even foreign exchange exposure. For example, if a U.S.-based parent company charges high management fees to its foreign subsidiary, it may drain cash from the subsidiary, affecting its ability to meet local obligations. Conversely, underpricing intercompany loans or royalties could lead to cash traps in low-tax jurisdictions, creating inefficiencies in global cash deployment.

A well-structured transfer pricing policy should align with the company's overall treasury strategy. This includes optimizing cash repatriation while minimizing withholding taxes and foreign exchange risks. For instance, some jurisdictions impose withholding taxes on cross-border payments such as royalties, interest, or dividends. Controllers must evaluate whether tax treaties between countries can reduce or eliminate these withholdings. Additionally, fluctuating exchange rates can distort the arm's length nature of intercompany transactions, requiring periodic adjustments to maintain compliance.

Cash flow forecasting becomes more complex in a multinational environment due to transfer pricing. Payments between related entities must be accurately projected to avoid liquidity shortfalls. For example, if a subsidiary is required to pay annual royalties to the parent company, the timing and amount of these payments must be factored into cash flow models. Delays in intercompany settlements can also create discrepancies in accounts receivable and payable, complicating month-end close processes.

Private equity sponsors often prioritize cash repatriation to service debt or distribute returns to investors. However, aggressive transfer pricing strategies aimed at maximizing cash flow can attract regulatory backlash. Controllers must strike a balance between optimizing liquidity and maintaining defensible transfer pricing positions. This may involve setting up centralized treasury functions, implementing netting arrangements to reduce cross-border payments, or using cash pooling structures to enhance liquidity management.

- Align transfer pricing policies with treasury and cash flow objectives

- Assess withholding tax implications of intercompany payments

- Incorporate intercompany transactions into cash flow forecasting models

- Evaluate tax-efficient cash repatriation strategies

- Monitor foreign exchange impacts on transfer pricing adjustments

TECHNOLOGY AND SYSTEMS FOR TRANSFER PRICING COMPLIANCE

Managing transfer pricing manually is a recipe for errors and inefficiencies. Given the volume of intercompany transactions and the complexity of compliance requirements, financial controllers must leverage technology to streamline processes. Enterprise Resource Planning (ERP) systems like SAP or Oracle can automate intercompany invoicing and reconciliation, reducing the risk of discrepancies. However, these systems often lack specialized transfer pricing functionality, necessitating additional tools.

Dedicated transfer pricing software can help controllers manage documentation, benchmarking analyses, and compliance reporting. These platforms often include databases of comparable transactions, making it easier to justify arm's length pricing. They also offer workflow automation, ensuring that documentation is updated regularly and submitted on time. For private equity-owned companies, investing in such tools can significantly reduce compliance risks while freeing up resources for strategic initiatives.

Data integrity is another critical consideration. Transfer pricing analyses rely on accurate financial and operational data from multiple entities. Controllers must ensure that data is consistent across systems and jurisdictions. This may require implementing data governance policies, such as standardized chart of accounts and intercompany tagging protocols. Additionally, robotic process automation can be used to extract and validate data from disparate sources, minimizing manual errors.

As regulatory requirements evolve, technology must keep pace. For example, the increasing emphasis on real-time reporting and digital tax compliance (e.g., e-invoicing mandates in Latin America and Europe) means that systems must be capable of generating and transmitting data in prescribed formats. Controllers should work closely with IT teams to assess system readiness and implement upgrades as needed.

- Evaluate ERP systems for intercompany transaction automation

- Implement specialized transfer pricing software for documentation and compliance

- Establish data governance protocols for consistent intercompany reporting

- Explore RPA for data extraction and validation

- Stay updated on digital tax compliance requirements and system needs

STRATEGIC CONSIDERATIONS FOR PRIVATE EQUITY-OWNED COMPANIES

Private equity ownership adds another layer of complexity to transfer pricing. Sponsors often prioritize tax efficiency and cash flow optimization, but controllers must ensure that these objectives don't compromise compliance. For example, aggressive profit-shifting strategies may yield short-term gains but invite long-term scrutiny. Controllers should engage with private equity stakeholders early to align transfer pricing policies with both financial and regulatory goals.

During mergers and acquisitions, transfer pricing due diligence is critical. Acquiring a company with non-compliant transfer pricing practices can lead to unforeseen liabilities. Controllers must review target companies' intercompany agreements, documentation, and audit history to assess risks. Post-acquisition, integrating the target's transfer pricing policies into the existing framework requires careful planning to avoid disruptions.

Exit planning is another key consideration. When preparing for a sale or IPO, private equity sponsors will want to present a clean transfer pricing posture to potential buyers or regulators. Controllers should conduct a pre-exit review to identify and rectify any compliance gaps. This may involve updating documentation, settling disputes with tax authorities, or restructuring intercompany transactions to enhance transparency.

Ultimately, transfer pricing should be viewed as a strategic tool rather than a compliance burden. When managed effectively, it can enhance profitability, reduce tax risks, and support global operations. Controllers who master this balance become invaluable assets to private equity-owned companies.

- Align transfer pricing strategies with private equity objectives

- Conduct thorough transfer pricing due diligence during M&A

- Integrate acquired entities' transfer pricing policies post-acquisition

- Prepare for exits by addressing compliance gaps in advance

- Position transfer pricing as a strategic enabler for the business

CHAPTER 17:

MANAGING RELATIONSHIPS WITH PE SPONSORS

• ◆ •

PRIVATE EQUITY SPONSORSHIP: A CONTROLLER'S GUIDE

Private equity sponsors are not just investors—they are active stakeholders who demand transparency, strategic alignment, and financial discipline. As a financial controller, your ability to manage this relationship effectively can determine the success of the portfolio company and your own professional trajectory. Unlike traditional corporate environments where financial reporting may follow a more predictable cadence, PE-backed companies operate under heightened scrutiny, aggressive growth targets, and compressed timelines. This chapter explores the nuances of fostering trust, delivering actionable insights, and navigating the unique expectations of PE sponsors. We will cover communication strategies, reporting best practices, conflict resolution, and the role of the controller in value creation. By the end, you will understand how to position yourself as a strategic partner rather than just a compliance officer.

Understanding the PE Mindset

Private equity firms invest with a clear exit strategy—typically within three to seven years—meaning every financial decision is evaluated through the lens of maximizing equity value. Unlike venture capital, which funds high-risk startups in exchange for equity, or founder-owned businesses that may prioritize long-term legacy, PE firms focus on operational efficiency, leveraged buyouts, and EBITDA growth. This distinction is critical for controllers because your financial reporting must highlight key value drivers such as working capital optimization, margin expansion, and capital expenditure ROI. PE sponsors expect real-time visibility into performance metrics, often requiring flash reports, rolling forecasts, and detailed variance analyses. They are less interested in historical compliance and more focused on forward-looking insights that inform strategic pivots.

To align with this mindset, controllers must adopt a commercial orientation, understanding how accounting decisions impact valuation multiples and debt covenants. For example, aggressive revenue recognition policies might inflate short-term EBITDA but could trigger audit red flags or lender and/or potential buyers' concerns. Conversely, overly conservative accounting may understate the company's growth potential, leading to misaligned expectations during exit negotiations. PE sponsors also prioritize liquidity management, so your cash flow forecasts should include scenario analyses for debt refinancing, dividend recapitalizations, or add-on acquisitions. The ability to articulate these dynamics in board meetings or quarterly reviews will elevate your role from transactional to strategic.

Another key differentiator is the level of involvement. While VC investors often take a hands-off approach unless milestones are missed, PE sponsors embed operational partners or interim executives to drive initiatives like cost restructuring or ERP implementations. This creates a dual reporting structure where you must balance the needs of the management team with sponsor mandates. Proactively aligning with both requires diplomacy—for instance, advocating for necessary system investments while demonstrating how they tie to IRR targets. Remember, PE firms measure success solely on investment returns, so your financial narrative should always link operational KPIs to equity value creation.

> *The best PE controllers don't just report numbers—they translate them into actionable levers for value creation.*

Finally, recognize that PE ownership is transitional. Your financial strategies must accommodate eventual exit scenarios, whether through a sale to another PE firm, an IPO, or a strategic buyer. This means maintaining "clean" financials with minimal adjustments, robust due diligence readiness, and a focus on quality of earnings metrics. Controllers who master this mindset nuances become indispensable during hold periods and exit processes alike.

COMMUNICATION STRATEGIES FOR TRANSPARENCY AND TRUST

Effective communication with PE sponsors hinges on clarity, consistency, and anticipation of their informational needs. Unlike public companies where earnings calls follow a set of guidelines, PE reporting is highly tailored and often demands ad-hoc analyses. Start by establishing a regular cadence of deliverables: monthly financial packages, quarterly business reviews, and pre-board meeting briefings. These should go beyond GAAP financials to include operational KPIs like customer acquisition cost, lifetime value, and backlog trends. Use dashboards with traffic-light indicators (green/yellow/red) to highlight areas requiring attention, but always pair these with root-cause analyses and remediation plans.

PE sponsors dislike surprises, so cultivate a culture of "no secrets." Bad news does not age well. If a metric is trending negatively, disclose it early with context—for example, a temporary dip in collections due to a client's payment terms rather than systemic issues. Frame challenges as opportunities: "While Q2 EBITDA is below plan due to raw material inflation, we've identified three supplier alternatives that could restore margins by Q4." This builds credibility and positions you as a problem-solver. Additionally, tailor your communication style to the audience. Operational partners may want granular details on inventory turns, while managing partners prefer high-level IRR sensitivities.

Technology plays a pivotal role here. Cloud-based platforms like Workiva or Adaptive Insights allow real-time data sharing and collaborative commentary. Implement a single source of truth for financial data to avoid version control issues during sponsor updates. When presenting, use the "Pyramid Principle"—lead with conclusions, then drill into supporting data. For example: "We recommend delaying the Midwest expansion by six months because [1] channel checks show softening demand, [2] construction costs are 15% above budget, and [3] our working capital line would be strained." This approach respects the sponsor's time while demonstrating rigorous analysis.

Conflicts are inevitable, especially when performance lags. When disagreements arise—say, over the allocation of add-back adjustments—anchor discussions in facts and precedents. Reference prior audit positions or industry benchmarks to depersonalize debates. If a sponsor pushes for aggressive accounting treatments, document the risks (e.g., "This could trigger a debt covenant violation per the credit agreement's EBITDA definition") and offer alternatives. Remember, your role is to be the steward of financial integrity, even when pressured to "make the numbers work."

Lastly, foster relationships beyond formal reporting. Attend PE firm events, understand their broader portfolio synergies, and occasionally share relevant industry trends. These informal touchpoints can pay dividends when you need sponsor support for a contentious accounting policy or system investment.

FINANCIAL REPORTING: BEYOND COMPLIANCE

For PE-backed companies, financial reporting is not just about compliance—it's a tool for storytelling. Your monthly and quarterly packages should answer three questions: Where are we against plan? Why are we there? What are we doing about it? Start with a succinct executive summary that highlights EBITDA, cash flow, and key variance drivers. Follow this with departmental P\&Ls, working capital trends, and capex spend versus budget. Use footnotes to explain non-recurring items like restructuring charges or one-time legal fees, as sponsors will scrutinize these during QoE analyses.

A common pitfall is overloading reports with data but lacking insight. Instead of just showing that DSO increased from 45 to 60 days, analyze the cause: "The increase stems from our largest client shifting to net-90 terms (impact: +10 days) and a one-time dispute with a distributor (impact: +5 days). We've renegotiated payment terms with the distributor and are offering early-payment discounts to others." This level of detail reassures sponsors that issues are understood and managed.

Debt compliance reporting warrants special attention. PE-owned companies often carry significant leverage, so covenant calculations (e.g., leverage ratios, fixed charge coverage) must be flawless. Create a separate schedule that reconciles adjusted EBITDA to GAAP net income, clearly listing add-backs with audit-supporting documentation. Proactively flag potential covenant breaches—if Q3 EBITDA is trending weak, model the impact on December's test and discuss preemptive waivers with lenders.

For exits, maintain a "data room light" year-round. This includes:

- Historical financials with audit reconciliations

- Customer concentration analyses

- Contractual obligations schedules

- Employee compensation benchmarks

- Capex and maintenance backlog details

When reporting to multiple stakeholders (PE sponsors, lenders, board observers), ensure consistency. Discrepancies between lender presentations and sponsor materials can erode trust. If adjustments differ (e.g., lender EBITDA excludes certain add-backs), document the rationale in both places.

NAVIGATING SPONSOR-LED INITIATIVES

PE firms frequently drive initiatives like cost reduction programs, ERP implementations, or add-on acquisitions. As controller, you are the linchpin for financial feasibility assessments and post-implementation tracking. For cost cuts, develop a savings tracker that quantifies initiatives (e.g., "Warehouse consolidation: $1.2M annual savings") and ties them to P\&L line items. Validate assumptions—if a sponsor proposes headcount reductions, model the severance costs and potential revenue attrition.

M&A activity is particularly intense in PE portfolios. During due diligence, prepare a quality of earnings package that normalizes EBITDA by removing owner-related expenses, non-recurring items, and accounting policy differences. Example adjustments might include:

- Owner's above-market compensation

- Discontinued product line costs

- Rent expenses for facilities not included in the transaction

Post-acquisition, lead the financial integration. Map the target's chart of accounts to yours, align revenue recognition policies, and identify working capital synergies. For system integrations, collaborate with IT to ensure GL mappings preserve historical data for trailing twelve-month analyses.

Sponsors may also push for dividend recapitalizations—taking on additional debt to pay shareholders. Model these carefully, stress-testing cash flow under different interest rate scenarios. Highlight risks like "If LIBOR increases by 200bps, our interest coverage ratio falls to 1.2x, breaching covenants."

CONFLICT RESOLUTION AND ETHICAL BOUNDARIES

PE's high-pressure environment can strain relationships, especially during underperformance. When sponsors demand unrealistic forecasts, resist the urge to acquiesce. Instead, provide a base case, downside scenario, and upside case with clear assumptions. For example: "Our base case assumes 5% organic growth, but if the new product launch is delayed (30% probability), EBITDA could be $2M lower. Conversely, if the pipeline converts faster, we could exceed by $1.5M." This probabilistic approach acknowledges uncertainty while maintaining credibility.

Ethical dilemmas may arise around revenue recognition, expense capitalization, or adjusted EBITDA calculations. Establish guardrails early:

- Document all non-GAAP adjustments with audit firm concurrence

- Require dual sign-offs on reserve policy changes

- Escalate unsupportable accounting positions to the audit committee

If pressured to cross ethical lines, frame objections around investor risks: "Capitalizing those R\&D expenses would increase EBITDA by $500K, but our auditor confirmed it would trigger a qualification, jeopardizing the refinancing."

Ultimately, the strongest PE controllers combine technical expertise with emotional intelligence. They understand that while sponsors drive hard bargains, their success depends on your ability to marry financial rigor with strategic storytelling. By mastering these dynamics, you position yourself not just as a steward of the books, but as a catalyst for value creation.

CHAPTER 18:

CRISIS MANAGEMENT AND CONTINGENCY PLANNING

• ◆ •

CRISIS MANAGEMENT AND CONTINGENCY PLANNING

In the world of private equity, the only certainty is uncertainty. A financial controller's ability to anticipate, mitigate, and navigate crises separates the resilient from the reactive.

> *Crisis management is not merely about reacting to emergencies—it's about proactive preparation, rapid response, and strategic recovery.*

In private equity backed companies, where financial performance is high-stakes and operational agility is non-negotiable, the financial controller plays a pivotal role in ensuring stability during turbulence. This chapter explores the frameworks, responsibilities, and best practices for crisis management and contingency planning from the controller's perspective, covering financial, operational, and compliance-related crises.

Understanding Crisis in a Private Equity Context

A crisis in a PE-owned company can take many forms: sudden liquidity shortfalls, regulatory violations, cybersecurity breaches, or even reputational damage from failed acquisitions. Unlike founder-led or venture capital backed firms, PE portfolio companies operate under intense scrutiny from investors who demand rapid returns, making crisis management uniquely challenging.

Private equity differs from venture capital in its focus on mature, cash-flow-positive businesses, whereas VC targets high-growth startups with higher risk tolerance. Founder-owned companies, on the other hand, often prioritize long-term vision over short-term financial engineering. PE sponsors, however, expect controllers to maintain rigorous financial discipline while preparing for worst-case scenarios.

The financial controller must identify early warning signs—such as declining EBITDA margins, covenant breaches, or irregularities in accounts receivable aging—and escalate them swiftly. Controllers in PE environments must also balance the demands of lenders, who may impose strict reporting requirements during crises, and equity sponsors, who prioritize asset preservation.

Key crisis triggers in PE-backed firms include:

- Rapid cash burn without corresponding revenue growth

- Failure to meet lender covenants

- Regulatory non-compliance (e.g., tax, payroll, or GAAP misreporting)

- Cybersecurity incidents compromising financial data

- Operational disruptions (e.g., supply chain failures, fraud)

Understanding these dynamics allows controllers to tailor contingency plans that align with sponsor expectations while safeguarding the company's financial health.

BUILDING A CRISIS RESPONSE FRAMEWORK

A structured crisis response framework is essential for minimizing disruption. The controller must collaborate with the CFO, legal team, and operational leaders to establish protocols for escalation, communication, and remediation. The first step is assembling a cross-functional crisis team, including representatives from finance, legal, IT, and operations, to ensure a coordinated response.

The crisis team should operate under a predefined governance structure, with clear roles: the controller typically oversees financial stabilization, liquidity management, and stakeholder reporting, while legal handles regulatory and compliance risks. IT and cybersecurity teams address data breaches, and operations manage supply chain or production halts.

Communication is critical during a crisis. Controllers must ensure transparency with PE sponsors and lenders while avoiding unnecessary panic. A well-crafted communication plan includes:

- Pre-approved templates for investor and lender updates

- Designated spokespeople to maintain message consistency

- Regular cadence (e.g., daily briefings for severe crises)

- Protocols for internal vs. external disclosures

Financial contingency plans should include stress-tested cash flow models to evaluate liquidity under worst-case scenarios. For example, if a major customer defaults, the controller must quickly assess the impact on receivables and working capital, then present options to the board—such as renegotiating payment terms or securing emergency financing.

Finally, post-crisis reviews are crucial. Controllers should document lessons learned, update internal controls, and refine forecasting models to prevent recurrence.

LIQUIDITY CRISES AND CASH FLOW EMERGENCIES

Liquidity crises are among the most immediate threats in PE-owned companies, where leverage is common and margins are tightly managed. Controllers must be adept at cash flow forecasting, identifying shortfalls before they become critical, and implementing stopgap measures to bridge gaps.

One of the first steps in a liquidity crisis is reassessing accounts payable and receivable cycles. Can the company extend payables without damaging supplier relationships? Can AR collections be accelerated through discounts or stricter terms? Controllers should also review contractual obligations—such as lease payments or debt covenants—to identify flexibility or renegotiation opportunities.

PE sponsors often require weekly (or even daily) cash flow updates during crises. The controller must ensure reports are accurate, granular, and actionable, highlighting:

- Projected cash runway

- High-priority obligations (e.g., payroll, debt service)

- Potential sources of emergency liquidity (e.g., asset sales, sponsor equity infusions)

In extreme cases, controllers may need to coordinate with lenders to waive covenants or restructure debt. This requires presenting lenders with a credible turnaround plan, supported by revised financial projections and cost-cutting initiatives.

Treasury management tools, such as automated cash positioning and scenario modeling, can provide real-time visibility into liquidity. Controllers should also maintain relationships with alternative financing sources, such as asset-based lenders or factoring companies, for rapid access to capital.

REGULATORY AND COMPLIANCE CRISES

Regulatory non-compliance—whether due to GAAP misreporting, tax errors, or payroll violations—can trigger audits, reputational damage, and even legal action. In PE-backed firms, where sponsors prioritize clean exits, compliance failures can derail sale processes or trigger valuation discounts.

Controllers must ensure that internal controls are robust enough to prevent compliance breaches. Regular audits of high-risk areas—such as revenue recognition, transfer pricing, or sales tax filings—can uncover vulnerabilities before they escalate. If a breach occurs, the controller's first step is containment: correcting errors, disclosing them to regulators if required, and quantifying financial impacts.

For example, if a company discovers it has underpaid state sales tax due to misclassified transactions, the controller must:

- Calculate back taxes and penalties
- Engage tax advisors to negotiate with authorities
- Update accounting policies to prevent recurrence
- Disclose the issue to PE sponsors with a remediation plan

Cybersecurity breaches, particularly those involving financial data, also fall under regulatory crises. Controllers must ensure that financial systems are protected with encryption, access controls, and regular penetration testing. If a breach occurs, the finance team must work with IT to assess data exposure, comply with breach notification laws, and safeguard sensitive financial information.

OPERATIONAL CRISES AND CONTINGENCY PLANNING

Operational crises—such as supply chain disruptions, fraud, or sudden leadership departures—can have cascading financial impacts. Controllers must integrate operational risk into their contingency planning, ensuring that financial safeguards are in place to mitigate disruptions.

For instance, if a key supplier goes bankrupt, the controller should evaluate the cost implications of switching vendors, including potential price increases or production delays. Contingency contracts or safety stock provisions can be prearranged to minimize disruption.

Fraud is another critical operational risk. Controllers should implement segregation of duties, regular reconciliations, and whistleblower policies to detect and prevent fraud. If fraud is discovered, the controller must lead the financial investigation, quantify losses, and strengthen controls to prevent recurrence.

Finally, leadership vacuums, such as the sudden departure of a CFO, can destabilize financial operations. Controllers should maintain detailed process documentation and cross-train staff to ensure continuity. Interim leadership plans, including pre-vetted external consultants, can bridge gaps during transitions.

In all cases, the controller's role is to ensure that financial operations remain resilient, transparent, and aligned with PE sponsor expectations—even in the face of crisis.

CHAPTER 19:

EXIT STRATEGIES AND PREPARING FOR SALE

• ◆ •

EXITS ARE NOT THE END

Exits are the culmination of years of financial discipline, strategic planning, and meticulous reporting. A well-prepared financial controller ensures that the company's value is maximized and risks are minimized during this critical transition.

UNDERSTANDING EXIT STRATEGIES IN PRIVATE EQUITY

Exits are the ultimate goal for private equity firms, marking the point where they realize returns on their investments. Unlike venture capital, which often targets high-growth startups with longer horizons, PE firms that acquire mature businesses typically plan exits within 3–7 years. Founder-owned companies, on the other hand, may exit through succession planning or strategic sales, often with less urgency. The financial controller plays a pivotal role in ensuring the company's financials are exit-ready, whether the strategy involves a sale to a strategic buyer, a secondary buyout, or an initial public offering. Each exit path demands different financial preparations, from audit readiness to structuring deal terms that align with GAAP and tax efficiency.

For example, a secondary buyout, where one PE firm sells to another, requires rigorous due diligence, clean financial statements, and robust EBITDA adjustments to justify valuation. In contrast, an IPO demands SEC-compliant reporting, often requiring restatements and enhanced disclosures. The controller must also differentiate between enterprise value (total company value) and equity value (value attributable to shareholders), as misalignment here can lead to disputes during negotiations. Additionally, controllers must anticipate earn-outs, deferred payments, or contingent considerations, which require complex accounting under ASC 606 (Revenue Recognition) and ASC 805 (Business Combinations).

Exit timing is equally critical. Selling during a peak EBITDA cycle or before major capex commitments can significantly impact valuation. Controllers should work with CFOs and FP&A Directors to model scenarios, including leveraged recapitalizations or dividend recapitalizations, which may precede an exit. A poorly timed exit, such as during a market downturn or before resolving audit qualifications, can erode value. Controllers must also ensure that all liabilities (e.g., pending litigation, tax exposures) are fully disclosed and quantified, as these become bargaining chips in negotiations.

- Review historical financials for consistency and accuracy

- Identify and document all contingent liabilities

- Align EBITDA adjustments with industry benchmarks

- Prepare GAAP-compliant pro forma financials

- Coordinate with tax advisors to optimize deal structure

FINANCIAL REPORTING AND AUDIT READINESS

A sale process hinges on the credibility of financial statements. Buyers and lenders scrutinize audits, so controllers must ensure that the last three years of financials are GAAP-compliant, free of material weaknesses, and supported by robust internal controls. Private equity sponsors often demand QoE reports, which dissect EBITDA sustainability, working capital trends, and non-recurring items. Controllers should preemptively address common red flags, such as inconsistent revenue recognition, unusual related-party transactions, or inadequate reserve policies.

For example, if a company capitalized routine maintenance expenses to inflate EBITDA, a QoE review would flag this as an adjustment, potentially lowering valuation. Similarly, controllers must reconcile differences between cash basis reporting (often used for tax purposes) and accrual basis (required for GAAP), as buyers will discount cash-based EBITDA. Another critical area is normalized working capital, which buyers use to peg the final purchase price. The controller must define a target working capital amount in the sale agreement and ensure the company delivers it at closing, avoiding post-deal disputes.

Audit readiness also extends to footnote disclosures. For instance, if the company leases facilities under ASC 842, the controller must ensure all lease liabilities are properly recorded and disclosed. Omissions here can trigger indemnification claims post-closing. Controllers should also prepare a data room with organized, searchable records—from general ledger details to contracts—to expedite due diligence. A disorganized data room signals operational inefficiency, which may lead buyers to question broader management capabilities.

- Conduct a mock QoE analysis to identify EBITDA adjustments

- Reconcile all balance sheet accounts before due diligence

- Document internal controls over financial reporting (ICFR)

- Prepare a comprehensive data room index

- Review all material contracts for change-of-control clauses

TAX OPTIMIZATION AND DEAL STRUCTURING

Tax implications can make or break an exit. Controllers must collaborate with tax advisors to determine whether an asset sale (taxed at higher ordinary rates) or stock sale (preferred by sellers due to capital gains treatment) is optimal. In PE-backed deals, buyers often push for asset sales to step up the tax basis of acquired assets, while sellers resist due to the tax burden. A hybrid structure, like a 338(h)(10) election for C-corps, can sometimes bridge this gap by treating a stock sale as an asset sale for tax purposes.

State and local taxes (SALT) add another layer of complexity. For example, if a company operates in multiple states, the controller must assess nexus issues and potential withholding taxes. Sales tax exposures, such as uncollected taxes on SaaS revenue, can become the buyer's liability post-closing, leading to price adjustments. International operations introduce transfer pricing risks; controllers should ensure that intercompany agreements and documentation comply with OECD guidelines to avoid penalties.

Deferred tax assets and liabilities also require scrutiny. If a company has net operating losses (NOLs), their usability post-sale may be limited under IRC §382, which restricts NOLs after ownership changes. Controllers should model the impact of such limitations on future cash flows. Additionally, transaction costs (e.g., legal fees, banker commissions) must be allocated correctly—some may be deductible, while others capitalize, affecting both GAAP earnings and tax liabilities.

- Model tax implications of asset vs. stock sale structures

- Review state nexus and sales tax compliance

- Update transfer pricing documentation for international entities

- Assess limitations on NOLs post-transaction

- Allocate transaction costs for optimal tax treatment

WORKING CAPITAL AND CASH FLOW CONSIDERATIONS

Working capital is a frequent battleground in exit negotiations. Buyers typically expect the target to deliver "normalized" working capital at closing, often defined as a 12-month average. Controllers must rigorously track metrics like days sales outstanding, days payable outstanding, and inventory turnover to avoid surprises. For example, if DSO spikes before closing due to lax collections, the purchase price may be adjusted downward to reflect the cash shortfall.

Cash flow forecasting becomes critical in the months leading to an exit. Controllers must ensure the company has sufficient liquidity to operate smoothly through closing, especially if the deal includes a cash-free, debt-free provision (where the seller retains cash and pays off debt). They should also model trapped cash scenarios—funds tied up in subsidiaries or restricted accounts—which may not be transferable at closing.

Another pitfall is earn-outs, where part of the purchase price is contingent on future performance. Controllers must establish GAAP-compliant methods to measure and report earn-out milestones, as disputes often arise over accounting judgments (e.g., revenue recognition timing). Clear definitions in the purchase agreement—such as whether EBITDA includes synergies or excludes one-time costs—are essential to prevent post-closing litigation.

- Calculate a 12-month working capital baseline

- Monitor DSO, DPO, and inventory trends

- Forecast cash flow through closing under multiple scenarios

- Identify and document trapped cash limitations

- Define earn-out metrics with unambiguous GAAP alignment

POST-EXIT TRANSITION AND CONTROLLERSHIP HANDOFF

The controller's role doesn't end at closing. A smooth transition requires meticulous planning to hand off financial systems, processes, and knowledge to the buyer's team. This includes documenting accounting policies (e.g., revenue recognition methods), system access (ERP, payroll), and key contacts (vendors, auditors). If the buyer plans to integrate the target into a larger entity, the controller may need to assist with GAAP alignment (e.g., converting from IFRS to GAAP) or system migrations.

Employee retention is another consideration. Key finance staff may be offered stay bonuses to ensure continuity, especially if the buyer lacks immediate replacements. Controllers should also prepare a transition services agreement (TSA), outlining which functions (e.g., payroll processing) the seller will temporarily provide post-closing. TSAs must specify cost allocations and termination timelines to avoid protracted dependencies.

Finally, controllers should conduct a post-mortem analysis to identify lessons learned. Did the data room preparation delay due diligence? Were there last-minute tax surprises? Documenting these insights ensures better preparedness for future exits—whether for the next portfolio company or the controller's own career advancement.

- Compile a transition binder with critical accounting policies

- Coordinate system access transfers with IT

- Negotiate TSAs with clear cost and duration clauses

- Recommend retention incentives for key staff

- Document post-exit lessons for future transactions

CHAPTER 20:

THE FUTURE OF CONTROLLERSHIP IN PE

● ◆ ●

THE EVOLVING ROLE OF THE FINANCIAL CONTROLLER

The financial controller's role in private equity backed companies is undergoing a seismic shift, driven by technological advancements, regulatory changes, and heightened investor scrutiny. No longer confined to traditional accounting and compliance, today's controllers must act as strategic partners, leveraging data analytics, automation, and cross-functional collaboration to drive value creation. Private equity sponsors demand real-time insights, predictive forecasting, and operational efficiency— expectations that require controllers to expand their skill sets beyond GAAP compliance and month-end close. The rise of environmental, social, and governance reporting, for example, has added layers of complexity, requiring controllers to integrate non-financial metrics into financial disclosures. Meanwhile, the accelerating pace of mergers, divestitures, and carve-outs in PE portfolios demands controllers who can seamlessly execute financial due diligence, post-merger integrations, and system harmonization.

The shift toward digital transformation is perhaps the most disruptive force reshaping controllership. Cloud-based ERP systems, robotic process automation, and AI-powered analytics are eliminating manual tasks, freeing controllers to focus on higher-value activities like cash flow optimization and risk management. However, this transition isn't without challenges. Controllers must now possess a working knowledge of IT infrastructure, data governance, and cybersecurity to ensure the integrity of automated processes. Additionally, the decentralization of finance teams—accelerated by remote work—requires controllers to implement robust internal controls and collaboration tools to maintain oversight.

Another critical evolution is the controller's role in investor relations. PE firms increasingly view their portfolio companies' financial leaders as extensions of their own teams, expecting them to deliver lender-ready reports, covenant compliance analyses, and EBITDA adjustments with precision. Controllers must also navigate the nuances of sponsor-level reporting, such as waterfall models and carried interest calculations, which differ markedly from traditional corporate finance. This demands fluency in PE-specific metrics like IRR, MOIC, and NAV, as well as the ability to communicate complex financial concepts to non-financial stakeholders.

> *The controller of the future isn't just a number-cruncher—they're a translator, a technologist, and a strategist rolled into one.*

Finally, talent development looms large. As the role expands, controllers must cultivate skills in leadership, change management, and cross-functional collaboration. The ability to mentor junior staff, manage outsourcing relationships, and align with PE sponsors' value-creation plans will separate exceptional controllers from the rest. Below are key competencies future controllers must prioritize:

Advanced data analytics and visualization (e.g., Power BI, Tableau)

- ERP implementation and optimization (e.g., NetSuite, SAP, Intacct)

- ESG reporting frameworks (e.g., SASB, TCFD)

- PE-specific financial modeling (e.g., LBO analysis, debt covenant testing)

- Cybersecurity and data privacy compliance

TECHNOLOGY AND AUTOMATION IN CONTROLLERSHIP

The integration of technology into financial controllership is no longer optional—it's a prerequisite for survival in the PE landscape. Automation tools like RPA and AI are revolutionizing routine tasks, from invoice processing to reconciliations, reducing errors and accelerating close cycles. For example, AI-powered anomaly detection can flag discrepancies in real time, while blockchain enabled smart contracts streamline intercompany transactions. Controllers must champion these initiatives, balancing cost efficiencies with the need for human oversight.

Cloud-based financial systems are another game-changer, offering scalability and remote accessibility critical for PE portfolios with multiple entities. However, migrating legacy systems requires meticulous planning. Controllers must assess data migration risks, ensure GAAP compliance in new systems, and train teams on updated workflows. The rise of "continuous close" capabilities where financial data is updated in near real-time also demands controllers rethink traditional reporting cadences to meet PE sponsors' appetite for timely insights.

Yet, technology adoption isn't without pitfalls. Over-reliance on automation can lead to complacency in controls, while fragmented systems across acquired companies create consolidation headaches. Controllers must implement robust change management protocols, including:

- Regular system audits to ensure data accuracy

- Cross-training staff to mitigate key-person dependencies

- Vendor risk assessments for third-party tools

- Disaster recovery plans for cyber incidents

Looking ahead, emerging technologies like predictive analytics will enable controllers to shift from reactive to proactive management. For instance, cash flow forecasting tools powered by machine learning can model multiple scenarios, helping PE firms anticipate liquidity crunches or covenant breaches. Controllers who harness these tools will become indispensable in driving portfolio company performance.

REGULATORY AND REPORTING COMPLEXITIES

The regulatory environment for PE-backed companies is becoming increasingly labyrinthine, with controllers at the forefront of compliance. Beyond GAAP and SEC requirements, controllers must navigate evolving standards like ASC 842 (lease accounting) and ASC 606 (revenue recognition), which demand nuanced judgments and detailed disclosures. International operations add another layer of complexity, requiring controllers to reconcile IFRS differences, manage transfer pricing policies, and comply with local tax regimes.

ESG reporting can be another potential challenge. Some PE firms face pressure from limited partners to disclose sustainability metrics, yet standards remain fragmented. Controllers must determine which frameworks (e.g., GRI, SASB) align with their sponsors' priorities while ensuring data integrity across voluntary disclosures. This often involves collaborating with operational teams to track non-financial KPIs like carbon emissions or workforce diversity.

Tax compliance is equally fraught. A potential global minimum tax (Pillar Two) and state-level tax law changes require controllers to maintain agile processes. For example, sales tax nexus rules vary widely, and missteps can trigger penalties. Controllers must also oversee R\&D tax credit studies, cost segregation analyses, and other value-creation initiatives that PE sponsors prioritize.

> *In PE, the controller is the last line of defense against compliance failures that can derail an exit.*

To stay ahead, controllers should:

- Monitor FASB/IRS updates through industry groups like FEI

- Implement centralized documentation for accounting policies

- Conduct mock audits to stress-test controls

- Engage external advisors for niche regulations (e.g., GDPR, SOX-like requirements)

THE CONTROLLER'S ROLE IN M&A AND VALUE CREATION

In PE, controllership is inextricably linked to M&A success. Controllers are critical in due diligence, identifying red flags like overstated EBITDA or weak controls that can sink deals. Post-acquisition, they lead financial integration—mapping chart of accounts, aligning policies, and delivering "Day 1" reporting. On the flip side, divestitures require controllers to carve out financials, ensuring clean separation without disrupting ongoing operations.

Value creation initiatives further expand the controller's remit. Whether optimizing working capital, implementing zero-based budgeting, or rationalizing cost structures, controllers must quantify impacts and track progress against sponsor milestones. For example, reducing DSO by reengineering billing processes directly boosts cash flow, a key PE metric.

Controllers also play a pivotal role in exit readiness. Preparing sell-side due diligence materials, ensuring audit-ready financials, and addressing QoE adjustments are all controller-led tasks that maximize valuation.

Key M&A focus areas:

- Pre-acquisition: Quality of earnings reviews, net working capital analysis

- Integration: ERP harmonization, synergy tracking

- Divestiture: Carve-out financial statements, TSA negotiations

PREPARING FOR THE FUTURE: SKILLS AND MINDSET SHIFTS

The next generation of controllers must embrace continuous learning and adaptability. Technical accounting expertise remains foundational, but soft skills like storytelling (to convey data insights) and stakeholder management are equally vital. Controllers should also cultivate a "private equity mindset"—thinking like an owner to align with sponsor objectives.

Professional development avenues include:

- PE-specific certifications (e.g., ACG's Private Equity Finance Program)

- Cross-functional rotations (e.g., FP&A, IT)

- Networking with PE deal teams to understand investment theses

Ultimately, the future belongs to controllers who blend operational rigor with strategic vision, positioning themselves as indispensable partners in value creation.

CHAPTER 21:

WRAP-UP

● ◆ ●

THE JOURNEY OF A FINANCIAL CONTROLLER IN A PE-OWNED BUSINESS

The journey of a financial controller in a private equity owned business is both demanding and rewarding. Unlike traditional corporate environments, PE-backed companies operate under heightened scrutiny, aggressive growth targets, and compressed timelines. As a controller, you are the linchpin of financial integrity, ensuring that every dollar is accounted for, every report is accurate, and every compliance requirement is met. This chapter consolidates the key lessons from this book, offering a roadmap to excel in this high-stakes role. Whether you are a seasoned professional or new to the PE landscape, these insights will help you navigate the complexities of controllership with confidence and strategic foresight.

KEY TAKEAWAYS FOR FINANCIAL CONTROLLERS IN PRIVATE EQUITY

1. Understanding Ownership Structures: Private Equity vs. Venture Capital vs. Founder Ownership

One of the first distinctions a controller must grasp is the difference between private equity, venture capital, and founder-owned businesses. Private equity firms typically invest in mature, cash-flow-positive companies with the goal of operational improvements, cost efficiencies, and eventual exit through sales or IPOs. Their involvement is hands-on, with stringent reporting requirements and aggressive timelines for value creation. Venture capital, on the other hand, focuses on high-growth startups, often in tech or innovative sectors, where the emphasis is on scaling rapidly rather than immediate profitability. Founder-owned businesses may lack the formalized processes of PE or VC-backed firms but often require controllers to balance the founder's vision with financial discipline.

Each ownership type demands a tailored approach. In PE, controllers must align with the sponsor's investment thesis, delivering detailed, real-time financial insights to support decision-making. VC-backed companies may prioritize burn rate management and runway extension, while founder-led firms might need help transitioning from informal bookkeeping to GAAP-compliant systems. Recognizing these nuances allows controllers to adapt their strategies, controls, and communication styles effectively.

2. The Pillars of Financial Controllership in PE-Backed Companies

The role of a controller in a PE-owned business extends far beyond traditional accounting. It encompasses several critical pillars:

- General Accounting & Month-End Close: Ensuring timely, accurate financial statements is non-negotiable. PE sponsors expect flawless closes, often with tighter deadlines than public companies.

- GAAP Compliance & Financial Audits: Controllers must maintain rigorous adherence to GAAP, as any missteps can derail audits or trigger investor concerns.

- Cash Flow & Treasury Management: Liquidity is king in PE. Controllers must forecast cash flows meticulously, optimizing working capital to support growth or debt servicing.

- Internal Controls & Fraud Prevention: Robust controls are essential to mitigate risks, especially during periods of rapid change or M&A activity.

- Stakeholder Reporting: PE sponsors demand granular, actionable data. Controllers must tailor reports to highlight KPIs, covenant compliance, and value-creation milestones.

In private equity, the controller's role is not just about numbers—it's about translating data into strategic

> *insights that drive investor confidence and operational success.*

3. Navigating Mergers, Divestitures, and Complex Transactions

PE-owned companies are often in a constant state of transformation—acquiring new businesses, divesting non-core assets, or preparing for exits. Controllers play a pivotal role in these transactions, from due diligence to post-merger integration. On the buy side, this involves validating target financials, assessing quality of earnings, and ensuring seamless integration of systems and processes. For divestitures, controllers must prepare carve-out financials, address stranded costs, and maintain transparency with buyers.

A common challenge is managing legacy systems during integrations. Controllers must evaluate whether to merge ERPs, retain standalone systems, or adopt new platforms—a decision that impacts reporting speed and accuracy. Additionally, transfer pricing and tax implications require close coordination with external advisors to avoid costly missteps.

4. Leveraging Technology for Efficiency and Insight

Modern financial controllers cannot afford to operate with outdated tools. Cloud-based ERPs (e.g., NetSuite, SAP, Intacct), automated reconciliation software, and AI-driven forecasting tools are no longer optional — they are now necessities. PE sponsors expect real-time dashboards, predictive analytics, and seamless data integration across departments. Controllers must champion these technologies, ensuring they align with the company's scalability needs.

However, technology adoption must be strategic. Over-customization can lead to inefficiencies, while underinvestment can hinder growth. The key is to balance standardization with flexibility, ensuring systems can adapt to evolving business models or regulatory changes.

5. Building a High-Performance Finance Team

A controller is only as strong as their team. In PE environment, hiring and retaining top talent is critical, as turnover can disrupt financial operations during critical periods. Controllers should focus on:

- Cross-Training: Ensure team members can cover multiple functions, reducing dependency on individual contributors.

- Continuous Education: PE dynamics change rapidly. Encourage certifications (e.g., CPA, CMA) and training on new accounting standards.

- Culture of Accountability: Foster a mindset where accuracy, timeliness, and proactive problem-solving are ingrained.

FINAL THOUGHTS: THRIVING AS A PE CONTROLLER

The financial controller's role in a private equity-owned company is not for the faint of heart. It requires technical expertise, strategic thinking, and the ability to operate under pressure. Yet, for those who master it, the rewards—professional growth, exposure to high-impact decisions, and the satisfaction of driving tangible value—are unparalleled.

> *Remember, your work directly influences investor confidence, operational success, and ultimately, the company's valuation. By embracing the principles outlined in this book—rigorous compliance, proactive stakeholder management, and relentless focus on efficiency—you will not only survive but thrive in the fast-paced world of private equity.*

The best controllers don't just keep the lights on; they illuminate the path to profitability and growth.

As you move forward, continue to refine your skills, stay ahead of regulatory changes, and build relationships with both operational leaders and PE sponsors. The journey is challenging, but with the right mindset and tools, you will become an indispensable asset to any private equity-backed enterprise.

ABOUT THE AUTHOR

•◆•

William Erosh is a retired senior financial executive and active consultant specializing in controllership and financial management for private-equity-backed and privately held small and mid-sized companies. Over a multi-decade career, he served in controller and senior finance leadership roles across diverse industries, often within PE portfolio companies undergoing rapid growth, operational change, or ownership transition. William has partnered closely with private equity sponsors, operating partners, executive teams, auditors, and lenders to design and operate finance functions capable of meeting institutional expectations. His experience includes acquisition integration, financial systems implementations, internal-control design, cash-flow optimization, budgeting and forecasting, and preparation for exits—all grounded in practical execution rather than theoretical models. Now retired from full-time executive roles but still consulting, William writes for finance leaders working inside PE-backed environments where clarity, discipline, and credibility are non-negotiable. His book series serves as a field guide for controllers and CFOs who must balance technical rigor with operational reality, helping finance teams become trusted partners in value creation.